Health, Wealth,
and the lifestyle to enjoy them.

Welcome to FinFit Life!

A letter from the President

There are many books that can have a positive impact on your life but very few that can be life changing. I am proud to say that the contends of the FinFit Life Blueprint when mastered and applied can truly be life changing for you and your family. Read it, study it, master it and apply it and you can achieve your biggest goals and dreams.

We are proud that you have chosen to travel this journey with us to create history as we disrupt an old industry while serving families. Our commitment to building health, wealth, and the lifestyle to enjoy both is a mission that needs leaders like you!

At FinFit Life we believe in entrepreneurship and the desire for someone to control and fulfill their own destiny. In addition to our executive team, we encourage you to work closely with your upline leaders on how best to apply these principles.

To your continued success,

William Pienias

President of FinFit Life

THE FINFIT LIFE BUSINESS BUILDING BLUEPRINT

FinFit Life is excited to provide this training manual to you, an independent contractor of this organization. As you know, FinFit Life operates through affiliated companies to make insurance, financial and other products available to independent contractors, such as you, for sale to the public. In addition, independent contractors are not required to purchase any products, goods, services, inventory, marketing plans or property of any kind, or pay any consideration in exchange for becoming or remaining an independent contractor of FinFit Life. However, all new independent contractors pay an administrative service fee of $100 in the United States to cover the costs of processing your application and coordinating license and appointment paperwork. FinFit Life processes all paperwork for licensing with all FinFit Life preferred companies. Finally, the compensation you will earn, if any, will depend solely upon your personal efforts and hard work. While many people have experienced successful careers within FinFit Life, these results represent individual experiences. As each individual differs, so will his/her specific results. Work ethic patterns, activity levels and dedication all play significant roles in determining the outcome that one may achieve and in his/her ability to control his/her destiny on an ongoing basis. This statement is not intended to nor does it represent that any current member's individual results are representative of what all participants achieve when following the FinFit Life Business System™. There is no compensation or consideration earned by independent contractors in exchange for encouraging others to join FinFit Life's sales force.

FinFit Life is not a franchise operation. FinFit Life simply provides you with access to a business system for you to execute and duplicate. Again, you are an independent contractor in business for yourself. The ideas and guidelines expressed in this manual are not mandatory but are merely suggestions based on what has worked for FinFit Life Associates in the past. You have the freedom to build your business within the framework of your contractual agreement with FinFit Life and the companies affiliated with the organization. However, remember that alignment creates velocity. FinFit Life is built on the "Team over Me" principle, and there is synergy in people moving and working together.

We are proud of this training manual and make it available to all FinFit Life independent contractors for educational and training purposes only. Illustrations in the manual of how attracting new Associates to expand your FinFit Life business can affect commissions of independent contractors are not a representation of past or projected future earnings of independent contractors.

No statement, illustration, graph or other representation in the training manual is intended to form a contractual agreement or modify or supplement any existing contractual agreement between FinFit Life and you. The terms and conditions of your relationship with FinFit Life are found in all contracts.

We are what we repeatedly do; excellence, then, is not an act but a habit.

– Aristotle

Our Vision

We believe there is no true fitness without financial fitness. That is why we are changing the way people understand fitness— by helping them make healthy physical, financial, and professional decisions.

Our Mission

To create a system that will help families grow their net worth, protect their loved ones, become healthier, and, for those who wish, build a successful business.

Our Core Values

Positive and Prepared	Driven to inspire others	Gets results
Lifelong learner	Grit and hard work	Do the right thing, the right way

Our Commitment to Helping All Families

Many families in today's world are feeling a serious financial pinch, with some even on the brink of financial disaster. We want to change this reality and make a huge difference in the lives of the people who encounter FinFit Life. We believe that families today have a desperate need for three things:

- Health - Simple ways to improve their health and incentives for healthier choices.
- Wealth - A financial education and plan to help them win in today's modern economy.
- And the lifestyle to enjoy them - A chance to take control of their lives by building a strong second income stream or a full-time business of their own.

If these three things resonate with you, and you like the idea of helping others while helping yourself and your family, then FinFit Life is for you!

With FinFit Life, you are in business for yourself but not by yourself. We are here to help you achieve whatever level of success you desire. If you are looking for success and growth, and understand that this often takes sacrifice, then it is time to take the next step forward.

TABLE OF CONTENTS

THE FINFIT LIFE **BUSINESS SYSTEM**

One of the most revolutionary businesses in modern technology, Uber, retains a model upon which a new generation of entrepreneurs have built a living — the "peer-to-peer" system. Their system provides drivers with not only a trusted name but with an entire system of doing business. A driver executes Uber's system, and the system itself will run their business. This model does not necessarily require talent, but rather, it calls for abilities that are easily learned and developed from that system.

The Uber system was built so that any entrepreneur can replicate over and over again, with each ride working as reliably and profitably as all those preceding it. To achieve success, the driver only needs to run the system and their business as it is designed. Many other businesses have become household names by following this same turnkey approach, such as Lyft and Curb; this ridesharing example teaches us how a business can use a system to make effective distribution a reality. For Uber, distribution meant bringing car service to the places where people who need it.

The FinFit Life Business Building Blueprint is your key to replicating this type of success as you build your business. It is based on the same time-tested principles that have built some of the largest companies across industries. Most people are more likely to succeed with a system in place to follow.

While FinFit Life is not a ride-sharing app, we have applied the same turnkey principles that make our system the solution that will bring you success. Become a student of the Building Blueprint and master it. Repeat the Seven Steps repeatedly, and you will realize unimagined success in your business.

FinFit Life allows you the freedom to build the business three ways - **One-on-One, Group, or Online.**

- One-on-One means meeting with people in their homes, restaurants, or places of business.
- Group means meeting with people in a group setting, whether in an office, hotel meeting room, or business center.
- Online means conducting business and recruiting in an online environment from your home, or anywhere you have internet access. This approach allows you to work one, two, or all three methods to build the lifestyle you have always imagined.

The FinFit Life Business System...

- Allows you to leverage your time to multiply your efforts and earnings.
- Allows you to spend time doing the work you love to do, rather than the work you have to do.
- Allows for duplication in others, so that the 1,000th leader is as effective as the first.
- Requires diligence and abilities that can be learned and developed, not special talents.
- Is driven by discipline and repetition.
- Is predictable, proven, and profitable.
- Is run by you, while the system runs the business.
- Requires courage, study, and grit.
- Is provided by experts in our field, along with any training you require.

To build a business that enables you to achieve your dreams, you must...

- Duplicate yourself and the system with your leaders to build an extensive distribution organization.
- Open new 'outlets' continuously to build your business.
- Learn and follow the Business Format System, to experience explosive, exponential growth.
- Work on your business, not in your business. Work on building a business, not on doing business.
- Build a "prototype" that can be duplicated.

Remember two things:

1. The key is to imitate and duplicate, not recreate the wheel. Follow the System. Do not deviate from it.
2. Marketing is the opening of outlets and the gathering of clients, simultaneously.

Become a Master Duplicator/Replicator

Repeat the FinFit Life Business System Seven Steps over and over again. The speed and precision with which you copy and execute the system will largely determine your success, and this same precision must be duplicated throughout your team.

You run the system. The system runs your business.

The FinFit Life Marketing Flow

The Business System allows people from all walks of life the chance to learn and duplicate a proven system. If followed and executed properly, it can help you build a business that will serve your life, not *be* your life. In addition, it will give you the tremendous financial and emotional reward of helping others.

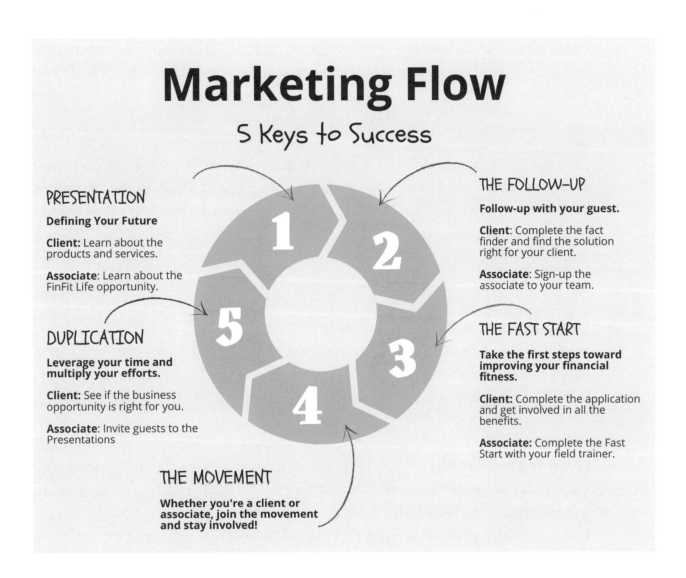

Marketing Flow
5 Keys to Success

PRESENTATION

Defining Your Future

Client: Learn about the products and services.

Associate: Learn about the FinFit Life opportunity.

THE FOLLOW-UP

Follow-up with your guest.

Client: Complete the fact finder and find the solution right for your client.

Associate: Sign-up the associate to your team.

DUPLICATION

Leverage your time and multiply your efforts.

Client: See if the business opportunity is right for you.

Associate: Invite guests to the Presentations

THE FAST START

Take the first steps toward improving your financial fitness.

Client: Complete the application and get involved in all the benefits.

Associate: Complete the Fast Start with your field trainer.

THE MOVEMENT

Whether you're a client or associate, join the movement and stay involved!

Keys to Success with FinFit Life

To get you started, here are a few very important things to keep in mind:

- First, understand how vast this market really is, and how perfectly positioned FinFit Life is to dominate that market. Once you clearly see the window of opportunity, it is up to you to determine how much of this market you wish to capture. Get a clear vision early in your career of how big you want your organization to be, then plan and work toward making your vision a reality for you and your family.

- Second, know that building a FinFit Life business will require work and effort on your part. Nothing worthwhile in life comes without effort, but at FinFit Life, we believe you will see a much greater return on your time and effort than in any other business we have ever seen. It will not always be easy, but we promise you it will be worth it.

- Third, follow our FinFit Life Business System. These proven, time-tested principles have built enormously successful organizations all over the world, spanning many different companies and industries. The key to growth in this industry is to create a system that others can duplicate.

- Lastly and most importantly, treat people as you would want to be treated. True success in life and business can only come through treating your leaders, teammates, and clients with honesty and integrity. Practice these principles every day, and you will build a business that you will be proud of, leaving a legacy for others to follow.

Traits of Highly Successful Financial Fitness Associates (FFAs)

How They View Their Goals

- Successful FFAs are on a mission – they decide what they can have, believe that they should have it, and then go and get it. No excuses.
- Successful FFAs have goals that far exceed others' expectations – assigned objectives are only the beginning.
- Successful FFAs are never content or comfortable with today's progress; they evaluate their performance and the quality of their activity regularly.
- Successful FFAs review their goals and measure their progress daily. They are disciplined even on a Friday afternoon.
- Successful FFAs visualize achieving their goals and are guided toward them by an internal compass.
- Successful FFAs celebrate victories. They remember to have fun and plan for it.
- Successful FFAs run marathons, not sprints.

How They Work

- Successful FFAs are scrappy.
- Successful FFAs start early every day.
- Successful FFAs sell during selling hours. Administration/housekeeping hours are before 8 AM and after 5 PM.
- Successful FFAs spend a minimum of 50% of their time outside of the office and 70% of the time selling.
- Successful FFAs return their calls quickly. Not every call, but every high-payoff call, usually from a cell phone.
- Successful FFAs look for efficiencies. They are consumed with finding a better way, not an easier way.
- Successful FFAs are always learning, and they learn by doing. They do their homework.
- Successful FFAs tell stories and are good at it.

What They Work On

- Successful FFAs know their product, their competition, and their market, inside and out. They know what others do not.
- Successful FFAs selectively quote. They analyze and pick every shot.
- Successful FFAs are calculated and work from positions of strength. They look for unfair competitive advantages.
- Successful FFAs look to be unique and search for unique opportunities.
- Successful FFAs focus on the selling process rather than the transaction.
- Successful FFAs thrive on new activity, not old.
- Successful FFAs make people feel their best in their presence.

Whom They Work With

- Successful FFAs do not discover clients, they create them. They fish in stocked ponds, not open oceans.
- Successful FFAs work exclusively with clients who will work with them.
- Successful FFAs know that some relationships come and go. They focus on those who have the passion to stick around and move quickly away from lost causes.
- Successful FFAs conduct a formal client needs assessment prior to making product recommendations.
- Successful FFAs are heavily networked within the industry and their community.
- Successful FFAs go beyond the product to provide their clients with value, integrity, and trust.

How They Think

- Successful FFAs never believe that they *cannot* or they *will not*. They just do.
- Successful FFAs are not consumed by what is on their desks; they are consumed by what is not.
- Successful FFAs have a decent boldness; they often say no but rarely hear no.
- Successful FFAs view their profession as challenging but not impossible.
- Successful FFAs play hurt.
- Successful FFAs are proud, determined, and appropriately entitled.
- Successful FFAs find success; they do not wait for it to find them. They depend on work, not luck.
- Successful FFAs have bad moments, not bad days.
- Successful FFAs fall in love with their clients, not their products.

How to Make Money as a Financial Fitness Associate

The FinFit Life Business System provides an amazing opportunity to build a second income business, or an entirely new career, in one of the most successful industries in the world. In the FinFit Life compensation system, you have five ways to earn compensation.

1. Personal Income

Every time you help a client and write new business, you earn a commission. As you reach certain promotion levels, your commission percentage increases. Because we encourage your Associates to reach out to everyone, not just high earners, there are no limits to how many people you can help.

2. Mentoring Income

Promotions open the doors to share opportunities and the position to train new Associates. As the Associates you train write new business, you earn a portion of overall commissions.

3. Expansion Income

There are no territories holding you and your business back. You are free to expand your business anywhere in the United States that you are licensed in. From a local team, to teams that you establish in other towns or other states, our platform will support your efforts and your organization.

4. Bonus Income

Qualified leaders earn a pro-rata share of an override on our entire company. Your portion of the bonus pool can grow based on your organization's production. Company-wide bonus pools can multiply and compound your earning potential, while rewarding leaders for the quantity and quality of their business.

5. Leaders Incentive Plan

Qualified leaders that build their business with us will have a unique incentive plan at FinFit Life. Ask your leader how to qualify.

The Three Exchange Principles

FinFit Life has a powerful set of values that are instrumental to your success and the success of your people called: The Three Exchange Principals. Using this method, you will do something once to exchange it for many. This is a great way for new Associates to learn from an expert at every step and then be rewarded many times over when he/she teaches these steps to his/her new leaders. You are essentially exchanging the education and the income from these activities for the right and privilege to teach others and receive income from the fruits of their learning activities.

1. Personal Sale Exchange

Your leader writes your personal sale. In exchange, this gives you the right to make personal sales to the people who join your team. In a sense, you are trading your one sale for the right and privilege to make many.

2. Field Training Exchange

Generate activity and learn from the best as you observe your Leader/Field Trainer make your training sales. This gives you the confidence that your warm market is dealing with the right experience and expertise. Then, once you are properly trained and licensed, you now have the right to make training sales for everyone who joins your team.

3. Promotion Qualification Exchange

Everyone must earn their promotion through the FinFit Life guidelines. In this way, you are setting an example for your people and gaining additional leadership power. You are not asking anyone to do what you have not already done to qualify for your position.

The concept of exchange principles is counter-intuitive for many individuals and certainly a point of contention for those in the traditional industry. These people commonly believe it is in their self-interest to hold off on selling products to their family and friends directly until they are licensed, instead of having assistance from their leader. They believe that by making the sales themselves, they will not have given up commission to their up-line.

This mentality is completely misguided for several reasons and is a big reason why studies indicate that 69% of agents fail in the first two years (per LIMRA).

There are several reasons why the Exchange Principles enhance the new member's opportunity for long-term success. First, no matter how much you read a book or watch videos, studies have proven that the best way for adults to learn is through active participation. While the company prides itself on having world-class training materials, there is no substitution for learning via personal mentor who you can observe in real situations. You would not have a doctor perform open-heart surgery on you if they only read a book without participating in actual surgeries with a mentor. Nor would you fly a plane with a pilot who had not gained experience as a co-pilot on actual flights. Dealing with a client's financial matters is no different. You need this training to become a professional and do the best job you can for your clients and team. FinFit Life requires a minimum amount of field training for all members (see promotional guidelines) for this reason and encourages this practice as much as possible.

Another reason why traditional thinkers resist exchange principles would be excessive ego. They believe they are too smart and talented to require field training. This too, is a big mistake. No matter your IQ or talent level, you will never know all the answers and you will lose the confidence of your customers by bluffing. Wise people gain insight from those with more experience (your up-line). Moreover, because your up-line receives an override on your performance, it would be foolish not to utilize them as a resource. Last, in abiding by the exchange principles, you gain the respect needed to lead others. As you build your team and train them, you cannot be a strong leader if you do not practice what you preach. How can you possibly have credibility by asking someone to do something you did not do yourself? You cannot.

THE SEVEN STEPS TO BUILDING YOUR BUSINESS

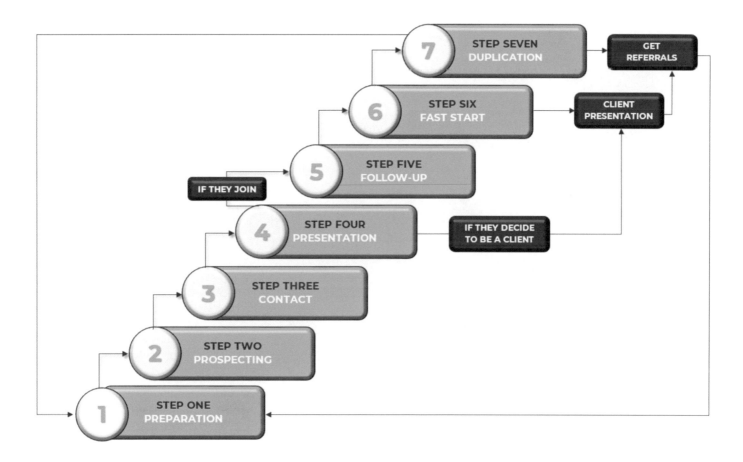

The rapid and systematic repetition of these simple steps will help you build a large, nationwide FinFit Life team.

By failing to prepare, you are preparing to fail.

– Benjamin Franklin

STEP 1 PLANNING & PREPARATION

Purpose: To make the plans and preparations necessary to achieve what you want in life.

Planning and Preparation are composed of **four elements**:

- Shaping a Successful Mindset
- Creating Your Personal Plan
- Creating Your Business Plan
- Putting Your Plans into Action

Planning and preparation are paramount to achieving success in both life and business. However, preparation goes beyond simply having your resources organized and gaining the knowledge required to succeed. You must also be mentally prepared with the proper vision and personalized direction to achieve your ultimate quest for physical, spiritual, and emotional success. This deeper view of success transcends material prosperity; rather, it allows you to focus on reaching that true peace of mind, which comes from winning in all areas of your life.

This step is the most important step in the FinFit Life system. By seizing this crucial moment, you can build the foundation and motivation needed to realize your purpose and identify your goals to support that purpose. This foundation will serve as the blueprint for your future success.

However, without this foundation, your chances of success in the business environment diminishes. You will be unable to apply the necessary effort and dedication required to implement the system with your personal purpose. You do not have clarity around what needs to be done to achieve your purpose.

Shaping a **Successful Mindset**

In order to truly succeed in life and business, you must shape your mindset and focus to support the habits and expectations that will last throughout your career. Several resources can help you develop a Successful Mindset, including the books you read, the audio you listen to, the videos you watch and the people you associate with in life. We will cover just a few of the ways you can start to develop a Winning Mindset.

We believe that leaders with this mindset are not just born that way, they are developed.

 It is important to know that real Leadership does not require specific talents – it only requires desire, learned abilities, and the willingness to think in new ways. Anyone who has the desire can learn, develop, and master the skills it takes to become a great leader with a great mindset.

You can and will become a great leader, who people will follow, if you are passionate about what you do. If you are willing to put in the time, effort and focus and treat people with respect, you will become successful.

Becoming a Great Leader with a Successful Mindset

It is important to realize that every great leader in history is just a person like you. They felt scared, frustrated, hurt, and worried just like everyone else. The difference is they go out and make things happen anyway. They do not search for excuses. They just find a way to succeed despite any obstacles that may appear in their way.

Great leaders exhibit these Successful Mindset traits that you must emulate:

- Accept responsibility and ownership for yourself and your life.
- Be focused and intentional every day.
- Be coachable and teachable.
- Stay positive and renew your passion, especially through the tough times. Avoid being a cynical, selfish, or pessimistic person. People create their own misfortunes due to the negative thoughts they allow to permeate the subconscious mind.
- Have a do-it-first leadership mentality and become a master copy worth duplicating. Your leaders are watching and they will duplicate everything – the good and the bad.
- Be a great follower. All great leaders were once and still, are great followers.
- Be persistent. Remember things are never as good or as bad as they seem. Never get too high or too low. Be steady through thick and thin.
- Work hard every day. Do not confuse motion with progress – if it is not making you money or moving your business forward, do not keep doing it. Do something that will.

- Be committed to pursuing your best self. Life is a continuous self-improvement journey.

- Discipline and accountability lead to growth and potential greatness.

- Be a professional in all that you do.

- Make every decision and perform every action with integrity. Treat people the right way always.

- Commit to doing things outside of your comfort zone.

- Practice what you preach; never be a hypocrite.

- Exercise self-discipline.

- Have a no-excuses mentality. You can make money or excuses, but you cannot make both.

- Develop resilience and be able to bounce back. Be gritty!

- Never let your personal problems and crises affect your people.

- Surround yourself with like-minded people who share your positive energy and passion for excellence.

- Dedicate yourself to being a servant leader. It is "Our" team, not "My" team. "We" have success, not "I" have success. Stay humble.

- Have a willingness to work hard every day.

- Remember that FinFit Life can change people's lives. Review our mission to understand why. Represent our brand and culture with pride.

- Focus on greatness, not just getting by. "Almost" is a way of life for many people, but not for a true leader.

- Understand that the difference between a good leader and a great leader is doing a little bit more.

- You only owe people two things – an opportunity and an example of success.

- Build a big team and make and save big money. Results give your leadership power. Success replaces all arguments.

Creating Your **Personal Plan**

Creating your personal plan is an exercise for which few people devote the proper time and thought. Studies have shown that people spend more time planning their vacation than their own life. However, having a personal plan can be the sole factor in determining whether a person succeeds or not.

Core Principles & Family Life Needs Analysis

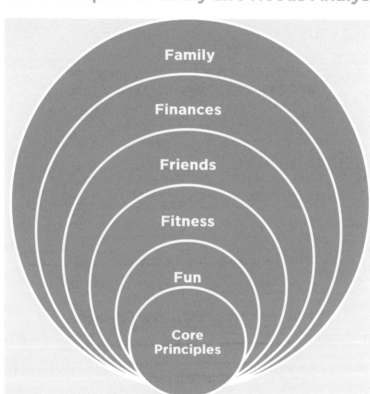

These five core principles—influencers, responsibilities, and commitments—determine the path we take, the pace we set and the sacrifices we make. These core principles are necessary for creating and maintaining a successful Family, Business & Individual life. These core principles drive the actions that will support personal growth within each of us.

Family

These are the people that support you on your journey through life and whom you are ultimately responsible for – your Spouse, Children, Parents, Relatives.

Finances

Successfully managing your financial fitness—income, lifestyle expenses, liabilities, protections, and retirement—is critical to advancing the other core principles.

Friends

Friends are the people outside your family that you have fun with. They are the folks you know, love, and care about.

Fitness

Your Physical Fitness is key to achieving holistic health. Commit to a healthy lifestyle, knowing the progress is more important than perfection. Remember, "Slow and steady wins the race." Use your Vitality subscription to make simple, healthy changes, and repeat these healthy habits every day.

Fun

What makes you happy? What makes you smile? What are the things you want to accomplish in your lifetime solely for you? What places have you always wanted to visit, things you have wanted to buy, experiences you have wanted to have? What are your personal dreams?

These Five Core Principles—when used together serve as your source of:

- **STRENGTH**
- **CONFIDENCE**
- **RESOLVE**
- **FORTITUDE**

Use the Core Principles & Family Life Needs Analysis found in your Starter Kit to establish and review your personalized results.

FINFIT LIFE

Identify what you want More of &/or Less of from each of the 5 Core Values.
Use the examples on the next page to spur your inspiration.

More of: Time, Money, Freedom, Balance, Commitment, Fun, Flexibility, Power, Strength, Joy, Significance, Excitement, Hope, Creativity
Less of: Restrictions, Tension, Complexity, Pressure, Stress, Confusion, Pain, Negativity, Hostility, Adversity, Suspension, Sarcasm, Fear

FAMILY	FINANCES	FRIENDS	FITNESS	FUN
More:				
Less:				

PERSONAL INTRINSIC PHILOSOPHY That which makes YOU --> YOU

My Purpose	My Stand	My Strengths	Spoken Epitaph
What do I want to do with my time on this planet?	How do I validate my purpose (the way I do things)	Skill sets/qualities that will enable me to fulfill my purposes and F-5 goals	What I want people to say about me at my funeral
If you had the power to erase a regret in your life, what would you erase? Why?	Who is the person (living or not) whom you hold with the greatest respect? Why?	If you won the lottery tomorrow, what would you do with the money? Why?	If you were diagnosed with a terminal illness, what would you do with your final year?

FFL-SG-82619V1   Draft Subject to Change

FINFIT LIFE

FOLLOWING IS AN EXAMPLE OF AN AGENT'S F-5 TO HELP YOU GET STARTED

FAMILY	By when	FINANCES	By when	FRIENDS	By when	FITNESS	By when	FUN	By when
Devote more time to my daughter	Now	Pay off credit cards	1 yr	Pay total cost of my 25 year class reunion	4 yrs	Drop 5% body fat	1 yr	See my birthplace	5 yrs
Begin her retirement account.	Now	Pay off cars	3 yrs	Golf trip to Scotland	4 yrs	Read more monthly	Now	Fit Camp	1 yr
		Pay off house	5 yrs					Dream Boat	5 yrs

PERSONAL INTRINSIC PHILOSOPHY That which makes YOU --> YOU

My Purpose	My Stand	My Strengths	Spoken Epitaph
What do I want to do with my time on this planet?	How do I validate my purpose (the way I do things)	Skill sets/qualities that will enable me to fulfill my purposes and F-5 goals	What I want people to say about me at my funeral
Be the driving force for my family	Do it right the first time	Tenacity	He lead by example
Inspire others to improve	Authentic speak	Leadership	He lived a life that others dream of
Become a role model	Think BIG	Organization	He provided for his family
Show my daughter the way to success	Find a way to win	Enthusiasm	He was a true teammate
If you had the power to erase a regret in your life, what would you erase? Why?	Who is the person (living or not) whom you hold with the greatest respect? Why?	If you won the lottery tomorrow, what would you do with the money? Why?	If you were diagnosed with a terminal illness, what would you do with your final year?
My career choice	Abraham Lincoln	Pay off all my debt	Seek to repair relationships
Apologize to my first wife	He was relentless in his pursuit of his dreams of success even though he failed many times over many different ventures. He took a stand against tyranny and the exploits of the status quo to do the right thing for people other than himself at the greatest cost.	Pay off my parents debt	Spend more time with family
Not serving my country		Begin an IRA for my children	Finally sky dive
Took my family for granted		Take a year off to sail around the world	Find my father
Picking on someone in school		Start a scholarship for veterans	

Your F-5 Core Mission Statement is your WHY. Identifying & combining your F-5 Core Values & Personal Philosophy into a single statement of action, which unifies your life mission fueling the confidence, resolve & fortitude to overcome adversity in the creation of a Bullet Proof Business Plan.

My mission is to lead from the front of the line. To utilize my gifts of teaching and leadership to create opportunities and advantages for those that are close to me as well as some that have never heard of me. With my skill set and opportunity laid before me, I am in a unique position to push my physical and mental limitation to greater level of awareness and lift those up around me who I wish to help and who are in need. I would like to stop paying interest to the bank and create investments which they pay interest to me. I have a burning desire to help some of my close friends with services that are important to them that will altruistically benefit others. To create residual income streams that will benefit my legacy.

FFL-SG-82619V1   Draft Subject to Change

The FinFit Life F-5 Worksheet

FAMILY	By When	FINANCES	By When	FRIENDS	By When	FITNESS	By When	FUN	By When

PERSONAL INTRINSIC PHILOSOPHY That which makes YOU --> YOU

My Purpose	My Stand	My Strengths	Spoken Epitaph
What do I want to do with my time on this planet	How do I validate my purpose (the way I do thing)	Skill sets I possess that will enable me to fulfill my purposes and F-5 goals	What I want people to say about me at my funeral
If you had the power to erase a regret in your life, what would you erase? Why?	Who is the person (living or not) whom you hold with the greatest respect? Why?	If you won the lottery tomorrow, what would you do with the money? Why?	If you were diagnosed with a terminal illness, what would you do with your final year?

Your F-5 Core Mission Statement is your WHY. Identifying & combining your F-5 Core Values & Personal Philosophy Into a single statement of action, which unifies your life mission fueling the confidence, resolve & fortitude to overcome adversity in the creation of a Bullet Proof Business Plan.

_____

_____

_____

_____

_____

AN EXAMPLE OF AN AGENT'S F-5 TO HELP YOU GET STARTED

FAMILY	By When	FINANCES	By When	FRIENDS	By When	FITNESS	By When	FUN	By When
Devote more time to my daughter	Now	Pay off credit cards	1 yr	Pay total cost of my 25 year class reunion	4 yrs	Drop 5% body fat	1 yr	See my birthplace	5 yrs
Begin her retirement account	Now	Pay off cars	3 yrs	Golf trip to Scotland	4 yrs	Read more monthly	Now	Fit Camp	1 yr
		Pay off house	5 yrs					Dream Boat	5 yrs

PERSONAL INTRINSIC PHILOSOPHY That which makes YOU --> YOU

My Purpose What do I want to do with my time on this planet	My Stand How do I validate my purpose (the way I do thing)	My Strengths Skill sets I possess that will enable me to fulfill my purposes and F-5 goals	Spoken Epitaph What I want people to say about me at my funeral
Be the driving force for my family	Do it right the first time	Tenacity	He lead by example
Inspire others to improve	Authentic speak	Leadership	He lived a life that others dream of
Become a role model	Think BIG	Organization	He provided for his family
Show my daughter the way to success	Find a way to win	Enthusiasm	He was a true teammate
If you had the power to erase a regret in your life, what would you erase? Why?	Who is the person (living or not) whom you hold with the greatest respect? Why?	If you won the lottery tomorrow, what would you do with the money? Why?	If you were diagnosed with a terminal illness, what would you do with your final year?
My career choice	Abraham Lincoln	Pay off all my debt	Seek to repair relationships
Apologize to my first wife	He was relentless is his pursuit of his dreams of success even though he failed many times over many different ventures. He took a stand against tyranny and the exploits of the status quo to do the right thing for people other than himself at the greatest cost.	Pay off my parents debt	Spend more time with family
Not serving my country		Begin an IRA for my children	Finally sky dive
Took my family for granted		Take a year off to sail around the world	Find my father
Picking on someone in school		Start a scholarship for veterans	

Your F-5 Core Mission Statement is your WHY. Identifying & combining your F-5 Core Values & Personal Philosophy Into a single statement of action, which unifies your life mission fueling the confidence, resolve & fortitude to overcome adversity in the creation of a Bullet Proof Business Plan.

My mission is to lead from the front of the line. To utilize my gifts of teaching and leadership to create opportunities and advantages for those that are close to me as well as some that have never heard of me. With my skill set and opportunity laid before me, I am in a unique position to push my physical and mental limitation to greater level of awareness and lift those up around me who I wish to help and who are in need_ I would like to stop paying interest to the bank and create investments which they pay interest to me. I have a burning desire to help some of my close friends with services that are important to them that will altruistically benefit others. To create residual income streams that will benefit my legacy.

BUSINESS BLUEPRINT QUANTIFYING TOOL

Establish what you want, for whom you want it, & what it is going to take to achieve it. THINK BIG you will be surprised how achievable your dreams may be.

Family

Buy new house, car, boat, clothes, College Funding, Vacation, and More Free Time

What are some items/activates you want for your family?

Items/Action	Time	Investment	Money

Finances

Spouse can quit job, supplement retirement strategy, pay off credit card debt, and consolidate student loans

What are some things you want accomplish to improve your financial position?

Items/Action	Time	Investment	Money

Friends

Wives Trip to Caribbean, Husbands Scotland golf trip, National Championship trip, and Concerts

What are some things you want to do socially with friends?

Items/Action	Time	Investment	Money

Fitness

Athletic Competition, College, Write a Book, reduce BMI and Train for a marathon

What activities/items do you need to do to be able to increase your fitness?

Items/Action	Time	Investment	Money

FUN

Become a Big Brother/Sister, Sky Diving, Quit Smoking, Lose Weight, Volunteer, or Travel

List activities you want to accomplish for yourself that will be fun before you die.

Items/Action	Time	Investment	Money

What needs to happen to reach your goals:

_____

_____

_____

S.M.A.R.T. Goal-Setting

Specific
- Goal setting only works if it is written down and communicated to others
- Define the goal as clearly as possible.
- Who is involved? What do I need to accomplish?
- Where will it be done?
- Why am I doing this?
- Which constraints and/or requirements do I have?

Measurable
- Can you track the progress and measure the outcome?
- How much?
- How many?
- How will I know when my goal is accomplished?

Attainable/Achievable
- Is the goal reasonable enough to be accomplished? How so?
- Make sure the goal is not out of reach or below standard performance.

Relevant
- Is the goal worthwhile and will it meet your needs?
- Is the goal consistent with the other goals you have established and does it fit with your immediate and long-term plans?

Timely
- Does your objective include a time limit? Example: I will complete this step by month/day/year.
- Will it establish a sense of urgency and prompt you to have better time management?

Creating Your **Business Plan**

Every Associate needs to create a lasting business plan to achieve their goals. An exceptional business plan helps you develop a clear, concise mental picture of what you want your FinFit Life business to give you in the short term and long term.

The Components of a Great Business Plan

- Set your exact goals for the size organization you want to build and the income you want to generate. Then break that down by the number of prospects that need to be seen and the number of leaders you need to build.
- Determine exactly how much time, resources, and effort you are willing to put toward achieving these goals.
- Set definite deadlines for your short-term and long-term goals and commit to them.
- Put this plan into writing. A goal not written down is only a wish.
- Begin at once. There is magic in taking action immediately. You want to have the leadership principle of the "Law of Momentum" on your side.
- Review your business plan daily and visualize what your life will be like when you achieve your goals.

Remember:

- Write deep and important emotions in your statement. Your "Why" should be etched into your brain and heart.
- Work with your leaders to set and achieve their goals.
- Maintain high, positive expectations and standards of excellence.

Putting the Numbers to It

Here is a rule of thumb that has always held true:

The average number of people you see per week—whether it is through Group, Online, or One-on-One Presentations— equals the number of sales you and/or your team will achieve in a given month.

While many people experience even better results than that, this general rule of thumb gives you a guideline in setting your goals for a given month.

Therefore, using this rule of thumb, if your goal is to have one sale a month, then you would need to see one person a week during that month. If your goal is to have 100 team sales in a month, then your team will need to see 100 people a week during that month.

Personal Cash Flow Goals

If you have a hypothetical sales target of $2,400 at a 55% contract, you would make approximately $1,320.   Two presentations a week = Two sales a month = $2,640 potential income*

Team Override Commission Income

Using a hypothetical sales target of $3,000 at a 15% override, you would make approximately $450 per sale. 10 team presentations a week = 10 sales a month = $4,500 potential override income*

The key is to make sure you arrange the right number of meetings and the right team size to meet your needs. By making these calculations, you will be in control of your income.

Putting Your **Plans Into Action**

Whether we like it or not, the world runs on money. You need money to live and accomplish your goals. Unfortunately, the vast majority of people settle for small amounts of money and therefore "shrink" their goals. As a business owner, you do not have limits.

Once you understand your Personal Mission and have identified your Five Fs, the next step is to develop your own financial plan to support your goals. FinFit Life helps you create this plan by using financial software that is designed to identify your areas of opportunity/growth, otherwise known as a Needs Analysis.

Financial Fitness Associates are not required to purchase any of the products that the company offers or represents. Individuals have varying needs and our products may not be suitable in all situations. Assuming there is a need, however, it would make sense that you consider the same products that you will present to your family, friends, and clients. It would be difficult to recommend a product or service to your clients that you do not believe in yourself, and there is no better way to demonstrate your belief than to "eat what you cook." If you do not believe in the products we represent, then you should seek guidance to better understand our products or reconsider your affiliation with the company. You will never be successful representing products you do not believe in, and our culture revolves around providing valuable products and services to assist important needs for our clients.

Conclusion

Preparation is the most important Step in the FinFit Life system. During this time, you will have the opportunity to discover your motivation, realize your purpose, identify your goals, and create the blueprint for your future success. Review your plans often and review the four key areas of this chapter to stay on track for your personal success.

The greatest leader is not necessarily the one who does the greatest things. The greatest leader is the one that gets the people to do the greatest things.

– Ronald Reagan

STEP 2 PROSPECTING

Purpose: To organize and generate a constant supply of quality prospects.

While many businesses today rely heavily on advertising or leads to generate customers and business, FinFit Life believes there is a more effective way. Relationship Marketing has proven to be one of the most effective ways of bringing a message or product to market. Building a business in warm markets, where there is an existing relationship, is a very successful and cost-effective method.

You will succeed in your warm market with a systemized approach. Your approach should not be personality-driven or vary from situation to situation. Instead, you must adopt a proven system that will give your team the confidence to follow through, every time. This type of system will generate results that are easy for others to duplicate.

Warm Market Prospecting

Warm market prospects could be friends, relatives, neighbors, co-workers, or other past and current business contacts.

New Prospect Development

These prospects are new contacts you will meet in daily life, through referral, or on the internet and social media.

Target Market Development

These prospects are people you do not know but belong to a market or demographic you wish to explore. You can think of these prospects as people you "meet on purpose." Identify a profile or community where you believe you will have success, and find ways to meet and engage those prospects. Research and planning are your best friends.

Your Personal Warm Market

It is critical that every new Financial Fitness Associate organizes his/her warm market in order to create their prospect list. Look at this list as the people whose lives you can change by introducing them to this opportunity and/or FinFit Life solutions. Every leader and client at FinFit Life was once just a name on a prospect list.

Those names represent lives that can change with our business and product. Build your prospect list with the people behind the names in mind.

Do not exclude people from your list because you think they are too busy or already have a successful career. You never know whether the opportunity is right for someone without discussion. Let them make that decision for themselves.

Another important note: it is not just whom you know that matters, but whom they know as well. Sometimes the timing may not be right for the person you know, but it could be for someone they know. The source for some of your best leaders will be people who do not join your business.

As the leader, you should sit down with each new Associate and his or her spouse to help create their prospect list. Not only will this exercise yield the most names, but it will also be a great opportunity to build a strong relationship as you get to know them better. Use the FinFit Life Memory Jogger to help you add as many names as possible to the list. Have your new Associate go through each job on the Memory Jogger and write down the first name that comes to their mind. Initially, focus only on the names—they can get the rest of the prospects' contact information later.

You will be surprised at the results you get from this exercise, as names will come to your Associate's mind that he or she may have never have previously considered. This exercise is a great way for everyone to create his or her initial prospect list. Go through the entire list to help them build a huge pool of prospects.

Memory Jogger   FINFIT LIFE

Use the FinFit Memory Jogger to help come up with potential prospects in your network!

WHO DO YOU KNOW THAT:

Wants to save money	Wants to make extra money	Is Entrepreneurial
Quit their job	Wants a healthier lifestyle	Is a Fitness Advocate
Works in healthcare	Is tech Savvy	

WHO ARE YOUR FAMILY AND FRIENDS:

Parents	In-Laws	Sisters & Brothers	Sister & Brother-In-Laws	Accountant
Aunts & Uncles	Cousins	Grandparents	Best Man at wedding	IT Service Person
Bridesmaids	Neighbors	College Friends	Nanny	Nieces & Nephews
Gym Friends	Boss/Partner	Work Associates	Manager/Supervisor	Maid of Honor
Co-Worker	Receptionist	Landlord	Personal Manager	Church Friends

WHO HAS A SPECIAL JOB OR INTEREST:

Accountant	Burials	Glass	Mortgage	Relocation
Advertising	Cabinets	Golf	Motel	Rental
Airline Employee	Carpet	Grocers	Motorcycles	Restaurant
Apartment	Caterers	Hair	Motor Homes	Retirement
Manager	Childcare	Health	Movers	Satellite
Appliances	Church	Heating & Air	Movies	School
Appraisers	Computers	Hobby	Music	Security
Architects	Consultant	Hospital	Newspapers	Signs
Artist	Contractor	Hotel	Nursery	Ski
Attorney	Crafts	Insurance	Nursing	Soccer
Auditor	Dance	Internet	Optical	Spas
Auto Detailing	Delivery	Landscape	Party Planner	Storage
Auto Parts	Electric	Laundry	Payroll	Plays sports
Auto Repairing	Engineer	Lawn	Pet Business	Taxes
Auto Sales	Executive	Lighting	Photographers	Telecommunications
Baker	Exercise	Limousine	Piano	Telephone
Beauty	Financing	Loans	Pizza	Television
Consultant	Fire	Locks	Plumbing	Theatre
Bicycles	Florists	Mail	Police	Towing
Boats	Funeral	Martial Arts	Printers	Travel
Books	Furniture	Management	Radio	Truck
Bridal	Gifts	Massage	Real Estate	University

Identify Your "Top 25" Prospects

Your immediate goal is a prospect list with a minimum of 100 names, to begin with, and growing from there. From those 100, we will identify the "Top 25." Here are nine attributes of a highly qualified prospect:

- 25+ years old
- Loves someone / Owe someone
- Dependent children
- Homeowner
- Good business background
- Good income ($70K-$100K) or substantial savings
- Dissatisfied with their current situation
- Entrepreneurial-minded / Interested in Financial Fitness
- Fitness enthusiast (or an interest in becoming more fit)

There will be exceptions to these guidelines, but in general, the more of these attributes a prospect has, the better their chance of success.

FINFIT LIFE

TOP 25 List

My Name: _____ My Director: _____

Date Completed: _____ Sen. to Director: _____

	First Name	Last Name	R/F/A*	Phone Number	Profile**	FITNESS***	Characteristics	Hot Button	Contact Date	VIP Attendance	Results	Comments
1					□1 □2 □3 □4 □5 □6 □7 □8							
2					□1 □2 □3 □4 □5 □6 □7 □8							
3					□1 □2 □3 □4 □5 □6 □7 □8							
4					□1 □2 □3 □4 □5 □6 □7 □8							
5					□1 □2 □3 □4 □5 □6 □7 □8							
6					□1 □2 □3 □4 □5 □6 □7 □8							
7					□1 □2 □3 □4 □5 □6 □7 □8							
8					□1 □2 □3 □4 □5 □6 □7 □8							
9					□1 □2 □3 □4 □5 □6 □7 □8							
10					□1 □2 □3 □4 □5 □6 □7 □8							
11					□1 □2 □3 □4 □5 □6 □7 □8							
12					□1 □2 □3 □4 □5 □6 □7 □8							
13					□1 □2 □3 □4 □5 □6 □7 □8							
14					□1 □2 □3 □4 □5 □6 □7 □8							
15					□1 □2 □3 □4 □5 □6 □7 □8							
16					□1 □2 □3 □4 □5 □6 □7 □8							
17					□1 □2 □3 □4 □5 □6 □7 □8							
18					□1 □2 □3 □4 □5 □6 □7 □8							
19					□1 □2 □3 □4 □5 □6 □7 □8							
20					□1 □2 □3 □4 □5 □6 □7 □8							
21					□1 □2 □3 □4 □5 □6 □7 □8							
22					□1 □2 □3 □4 □5 □6 □7 □8							
23					□1 □2 □3 □4 □5 □6 □7 □8							
24					□1 □2 □3 □4 □5 □6 □7 □8							
25					□1 □2 □3 □4 □5 □6 □7 □8							

* R/F/A -- (R) relative (F) friend (A) acquaintance

** Profile -- 1. Over 25+ Years 2. Married 3. Children 4. Homeowner 5. Good Job/profession 6. Income over 35k 7. Dissatisfied 8. Entrepreneurial

***FITNESS -- 1. Fitness minded 2. nsurance industry 3. Teacher/coach/trainer 4. Network marketing 5. Enthusiastic 6. Sales 7. Self Employed

Build Your List Through Social Media Prospecting

In this digital age, there are many different social media platforms - Facebook, Instagram, Twitter, Pinterest, LinkedIn, and others—that we can use to our advantage. Start by signing up for 2-3 social media platforms if you have not already.

Once you have signed up, make sure you enter your personal information, including education and employment history. These sites use your data to connect you with the right people and people you may know.

Follow and add the suggested accounts to your friends list. You can also search by name and location to find contacts. Another way of growing your contacts is to click on the friends lists of your friends to find more people you know.

Keep your page centered on your personal life, not your business life. It is reasonable to share business posts on your profile, but only 2-3 times per week. Otherwise, you risk alienating your friends and followers.
We will show you how to approach people that you have become reacquainted with through social media in Step 3: "Contact".

Development of New Prospects

It is very important to continue building your prospect list by consistently adding new people. You will meet new people in various ways, including personal contact, referrals, the internet, and social media. Continue to follow the tips and guidelines below to maximize your new prospecting efforts.

Personal Contact

As you are out and about, there are always opportunities to meet new people to add to your prospect list. Some of these people will be candidates for your business and others will become referral resources. When you meet someone, keep the basic recruiting principles in mind. The key to developing new prospects is to be natural. Do not overwhelm them by saying too much.

Instead, your goal is to convince them to attend a presentation or webinar, or at the very least, view a recorded Corporate Overview.

Using the F.O.R.M. Method

F.O.R.M. is an easy-to-remember method for starting conversations and turning strangers into friends. Each letter represents a different topic you can use to start an easy conversation.

F - **Stands for Family** - Ask about their family and tell them a little about yours.

O - **Stands for Occupation** - Ask what they do for a living.

R - **Stands for Recreation** - Ask what they do for fun and discuss shared interests.

M - **Stands for Message** – Leave them with a brief message that sparks their interest in viewing the Corporate Overview.

Your goal is to make a good first impression and obtain their contact information.

The Power of "Friendship Networking"

You can also expand your warm market through Friendship Networking. This is a great technique to use in spare moments during your day to meet new people. The key is to be as natural as you would be while shopping or simply passing time.

Keys to Friendship Networking
- Do not approach people about the business when you first meet them.
- Understand and leverage "The Law of Averages."
- Remember that people need our opportunity to make either a serious second income or a career change. Meeting you (first) and learning the FinFit Life story (later) could be a life-changing experience for them.

How Friendship Networking Works

Where: Retail stores and small businesses.

When: The best times are between 9:30-11:45 am and between 1:15-5 pm when most businesses are the least busy.

How: Walk into the business and start looking around. The person in the store will usually ask, "Can I help you?" You then say –

> *"No, thank you. I have an appointment nearby and I arrived a little early. I am just killing a few minutes until it is time. This is a nice store — are you the owner?"*

The person usually is not but wishes they were, and this question usually gets them associating.

Then use the F.O.R.M. Method to get a casual conversation going while you are still browsing. Use questions such as: "Have you worked here long?" or "Do you live close by?" etc.

Stay there for no longer than three to five minutes. Your main goal is to get their contact information. As you leave, ask if they have a business card or write down their name, number, and the locations of their store.

The Friendship Networking Follow-Up

Call your new contact back in two days at their work or cell number, or visit the store again. Calling back the next day will appear too anxious. Waiting three days to call is too long, and the person may not remember you.

Say to him/her:

"Hello, _____. This is _____. I am not sure if you remember me, but I was in your store the other day and we talked about _____." (Use a subject from your "F.O.R.M." Discussion)

Listen, the reason I am calling is that I am working with a fast-growing company that is expanding in this area, and we are looking for people who have an interest in making a serious second income or a possible career change.

"Now, I do not like running ads or posting positions online because you never know who is going to respond, but you seem like the type of person we are looking for. I would like to text you a link to a brief video so you can see if you have an interest. Worst case, you may know someone like yourself who may be interested. What is the best number to text this to you?"

Next, send the contact message found in Step 3. Then contact them and follow the system from there.

Possibility Projections from Friendship Networking

If you spend 4-6 hours friendship networking, you can usually pick up 40-50 business cards/names.

If we use a very low average success rate, 40-50 calls should yield 20-30 people who will allow you to send them the video. You could then expect 7 to 10 of those people to see the Corporate Overview, whether in a One-on-One, Group, or Online setting.

Using these low, conservative averages: if only one of the 7-10 people who view the Corporate Overview joins the business, you would enroll one personal recruit per 4-6 hours spent friendship networking! If you did this five days per week, for four weeks, that would total 20 personal Associates in one month!

Many people will have better results than this. Still, this shows that even if you are not very efficient at friendship networking, you can use the "Law of Averages" to add new leaders to your team. Generally, there is no excuse for not knowing or finding people that you can recruit to your business.

Overcoming Questions While Friendship Networking

Some people may ask, "What does your company do?" You must be careful with your response to not say too much while not sounding elusive.

Sample Script:

> *"We show people how to make and save more money, while helping them to live a longer, healthier life. I do not have time to get into all the details right now, but if you would like to know more, I would be glad to send you an email that will explain it to you. What is the best number to send you a text message?"*

Do not go into any further details. You do not want to give too much away too early!

Using Warm Market Referrals

Warm market referrals are another way to expand your prospect list. These referrals are sourced from contacts you have already met, with whom you have forged some form of relationship.

The Importance of Referrals

You will encounter people while building your business who are not immediately interested. They can still be a great source of warm-market referrals for you.

Who Are Your Best Referral Sources?

1. Your natural market
2. Your clients
3. Acquaintances
4. Co-workers or business colleagues

The only way to get referrals is to ask for them. Keep in mind: you may want to ask more than once. While a person may not know someone who could use your services right now, they may in the future.

It is very important to do your research. Review your prospect's LinkedIn and Facebook connections. It might be best to suggest a referral.

For example:

> *"I noticed you are connected on LinkedIn with John/Jane Smith. I have been trying to find someone who could introduce me to him/her, can you do me a favor and text John/Jane, tell him/her that I am going to be contacting him/her and recommend that her/she meet with me?"*

Obtaining Referrals During the Contact Step

A great time to get referrals is after the initial contact has been made. If the prospect is not interested in attending a presentation or exploring the option of becoming a customer, they can still be a great referral source.

Sample Script:

> *"I appreciate how you feel, but let me ask you a quick question. I have found my best new Associates and Clients come through referrals from quality people like you. Who do you know that may be interested in getting involved in a new business venture or a possible career change?"*

Getting Referrals during the Presentation Step

If the prospect has seen the CORPORATE OVERVIEW, whether at the office, one-on-one, or online, and is not interested in signing up, there is still a great chance to get referrals.

Sample Script:

> *"I appreciate the opportunity to meet with you today. As you can tell, FinFit Life is committed to helping people achieve a better life through financial fitness and physical fitness. _____ (His or her name), I have built my business on referrals from quality people like you. Would you be kind enough to write down the names of a few people who you think might benefit from what FinFit Life has to offer?"*

Obtaining Referrals After the Client Presentation

The Client Presentation is one of the best times to get referrals. Once prospects have seen the power of FinFit Life and how it can help people achieve financial independence, they will realize that it is an important opportunity to share with others.

Sample Script:

> *"As you can tell, these concepts will have a dramatic impact on your finances and help you create a better future for you and your family. The amazing part is that most people have never even heard of FinFit Life. Who are some people you know who should at least have the chance to hear about FinFit Life, so they can have the same opportunity to learn about it as you did?"*

Overcoming Possible Objections in the Referral Process

Here are some of the common objections you may encounter when asking for referrals:

- Some people may feel they could upset their friends and relatives by providing their name as a referral. This objection is common among those who have dealt with overly aggressive salespeople in the past. It is important for you to communicate that you will not pressure anyone. Ensure that you will treat their referrals with the same respect you have given them. You will deliver the information they need to make the right decision.

- Some people will disqualify certain people to refer by making their own pre-judgments. It is important to remind them that FinFit Life has broad appeal for anyone who wants to get their financial house in order. It is important to tell your clients not to prejudge anyone, but let each person decide whether they want to hear about FinFit Life. Common questions include:

  o Who is the best businessperson you know personally?
  o Do you know anyone who exercises or works at a fitness center?
  o Who do you know who has kids that will attend high school or college soon?

- Some people may claim they cannot think of anyone. While no one may come to mind now, they know more people than they realize. This is where they can use the FinFit Life Memory Jogger to refresh their memory.

Once you master overcoming objections, you will have a successful turnkey method for obtaining referrals at each step, helping to build your FinFit Life business.

Contacting the New Referrals

There are two effective methods for contacting new referrals:

Direct Phone Contact for Referrals

Sample Phone Script:

> *"Hello, _____, [his or her name]. I am a friend of _____ [referrer's name] and I recently shared a concept with them that they were excited about. They liked what we are doing to help families build a better plan for the future, and were kind enough to mention that you might be interested in hearing about this as well. There are two ways that I could share this information with you. Either I can set up an appointment to come by your home, or we have a group presentation on Tuesday night at 7:30. Which of these two ways works best for you?"*

Set a time for the appointment or give the referral directions to the location of the group presentation. If they do not commit to a meeting, you can invite them to a webinar or, at the very least, send them a link to the online presentation.

Note: Make sure you are aware of any laws concerning cold calling and do not violate these laws.

Text Message Contact for Referrals

Sample message:

> *"Dear _____, [his or her name]. I am a friend of _____ [referrer's name] and I recently shared a concept with them that they were excited about. They really liked what we are doing to help families build a better financial plan for the future, and were kind enough to mention that you might be interested in hearing more about it, too. There are two ways that I could share this information with you. Either I can set up an appointment to come by your home, or we have a group presentation on Tuesday night at 7:30. Which of these two ways works best for you?*
> *I look forward to hearing back from you, _____ [Your name]"*

If the person replies and does not commit to a meeting, you can invite them to a webinar or, at the very least, send them a link to the introductory video or the full CORPORATE OVERVIEW video.

Cold Market Prospecting

If you have exhausted your warm market options and/or did not receive referrals along the way, there is always the option of cold market prospecting. We do not recommend it over a warm market, but it can work when necessary. There are a few ways to prospect in a cold market.

Local Business Meetings & Mixers

Business networking through meetings and mixers is a good source for potential Associates and leads. Keep in mind that most people in attendance are seeking new business contacts as you are. Effective networking means providing value and referrals to others first and obtaining referrals from them in return.

Types of Meetings & Mixers:

- **Local Business Mixers, Professional Groups, and Networking Groups** – As a visitor, you are welcomed at the monthly Chamber of Commerce Mixers and weekly networking groups. There are networking groups everywhere. You only need to ask around or perform an online search. These groups will look at you as a potential member, and you can always join them. Your initial purpose is to network and elicit interest in your business. There are also professional groups for Realtors, Brokers, Title Agents, Bankers, Contractors, etc.

- **Fitness Clubs** – You can set up tables inside clubs, or give an informational seminar to their members on how financial fitness is as important as physical fitness. Fitness centers such as Lifetime Fitness, YouFit or Planet Fitness are always looking to bring in value-adding events for their members.

- **Online Meeting Directories** – Find local meetings by searching online meeting directories such as EventBrite or Meetup. Take advantage and sign up for these free services.

- **Trade Shows & Community Events** – If you have an outgoing personality, are willing to stand in a booth all day and are willing to invest the time/money, Trade Shows and Community Events can be another source of leads for your business. You can also meet people by simply attending these events.

- **Home Events** – Your clients hold a meeting for their friends to share the information in a low-key social setting within their home.

- **Group Organizations** – Rotary, Lions, Junior League, Habitat for Humanity, Toastmasters, or other charitable organizations. **However, we would advise you to leverage these organizations cautiously, and only if they are an organization you already personally support.**

At events like these, use the F.O.R.M. Method to start a conversation and build rapport. Once it is appropriate to mention your business — or if they ask — one was to respond is:

"I own a financial services business. There is a lot to it but I specialize in counseling professionals who already assume their finances and retirement are on track. I help them to identify gaps, overlooks and shortcuts that they are unaware of and teach then new strategies than they can apply. I know that doesn't give you many specifics, but if you would like I could email (or text) you some things that would better explain it." (Wait for answer)

Advertising

Although FinFit Life believes strongly in the success and ROI of Relationship Marketing, you may consider advertising to a cold market. Your message does not necessarily need to cost money. If you do decide to spend money, your exposure and chances for interest and calls will match what you spend.

FinFit Life Compliance must approve advertising before you deploy it. All advertising must satisfy legal and marketing guidelines, which have been written for your benefit as well. **Do not depict opportunities at FinFit Life as salaried positions.**

Advertising Resources:

- **Free Online Job Boards** – Perform an online search for Free Online Job Boards and you will find both local and national websites where you can post simple "business opportunity" or "commission sales" listings.

- **Paid Online Job Boards** – These include sites such as Indeed.com, Glassdoor.com, LinkedIn.com, Monster.com, TheLadders.com, etc. It is expensive to post a listing. This kind of advertising is best for the more experienced recruiter, as you could spend money only to get poor results.

- **Newspaper/Magazine Advertising** – Simple advertisements in newspapers or cultural events publications have shown an occasional success.

- **Social media platforms** – Facebook, LinkedIn, Instagram, TikTok, Twitter and YouTube, etc.

Advertising Do's and Don'ts:

When advertising for new FinFit Life associates, you must avoid using phrases such as:

- Hiring
- Employment
- Part-time employment
- Salary
- Wages
- Steady work

Instead use phrases such as:

- Looking for partners/ sales professionals/ team leaders
- Looking for independent contractors
- Commission based earnings

Conclusion

Execute the prospecting methods in this chapter properly, and you will never have to purchase leads or work in a cold market. Relationship Marketing is the key to a successful marketing organization with leaders who can duplicate your strategy. Remember: everyone prefers to do business with people they know, like and trust.

The best way to predict your future is to create it.

– Abraham Lincoln

STEP 3 CONTACT

Purpose: To learn how to effectively approach and contact a prospect so that they can connect with the FinFit Life story.

Key Points: *Quick and Simple. It is an INVITATION not a PRESENTATION.*

The Importance of **the Contact**

Mastering an effective contact using proven FinFit Life methods will add to your confidence and help build your business. Contacting is among the most important steps of the FinFit Life Business System. You must master and internalize your own contact strategy first, then teach your leaders to do the same. Ninety percent (90%) of sales and recruiting failures occur during this step.

Give prospects just enough information to intrigue them about FinFit Life, without giving too much away. Too much information may cause them to jump to conclusions and not see the full FinFit Life presentation.

The Contacting Basics

PERSONAL CONTACT

Mastering a quality invitation is the proven method of avoiding the number 1 killer of success in FinFit Life, the "Scenario of Disaster." Always remember you <u>MUST</u> control the point of contact.

SCENARIO OF DISASTER

- o Your **ENTHUSIASM**
- o Creates **CURIOSITY**
- o They ask **QUESTIONS**
- o You attempt to **ANSWER** questions
- o You answer **WRONG**, from incorrect or incomplete information
- o They jump to **CONCLUSIONS**
- o The result is **FAILURE**

Understanding Human Nature

It is important to understand the natural tendencies of people when making contact. Become a student of human nature and become a "Fisher of Men."

Key Points of Understanding Human Nature

People typically:

- Jump to quick conclusions.
- Are skeptical.
- Procrastinate.
- Have big dreams and goals.
- Are naturally curious.
- Do not think they can sell.
- Do not like salespeople.
- Would like to be their own boss.
- Would like to have a business of their own, but ... doubt that they ever could or would.

The Seven Steps of the FinFit Life Business System will help you navigate through these natural tendencies so that you can help the prospect to see the opportunity with an open mind. This gives them the best chance for success. When contacting a prospect, remember to stick to the 10/50/50 rule: you have 10 seconds to earn the next 50 seconds and you have that 50 seconds to earn a 50-minute appointment.

There are many proven methods and scripts you may use to successfully contact your prospects. It is encouraged that you work with your Director, and trainer, to practice the words of the business together. Role playing is key.

Our business is a business of words. When you have the right words, and they are spoken with confidence, you will have success.

ETHOR

Once you develop your Top 25 list, you will want to contact each person as soon as possible to schedule a time to meet with them and share the information about FinFit Life. One method and a way of securing appointments to meet prospects, while taking the pressure off him/her, is by using ETHOR, which stands for:

I'm	**E**	**EXCITED**
I'm in	**T**	**TRAINING**
I need your	**H**	**HELP**
I value your	**O**	**OPINION**
Ask for	**R**	**REFERRALS**

Keep it simple.

Keep it short.

Be direct.

You do not need to justify or explain the time you are requesting, as it is important to you and you value their feedback and opinion. Most people, even strangers, are willing to help you if you ask!

TRUST – CREDIBILITY – RESPECT TRIANGLE

Leader / Trainer and New Associate act as joint inviter

As a new associate starting in a brand new industry, it is strongly encouraged and recommended that you work with your Director and experienced trainer to help create a successful connection with your prospects. This is true especially with your own friends and family.

You = Trust

Trainer = Credibility

Together = Success

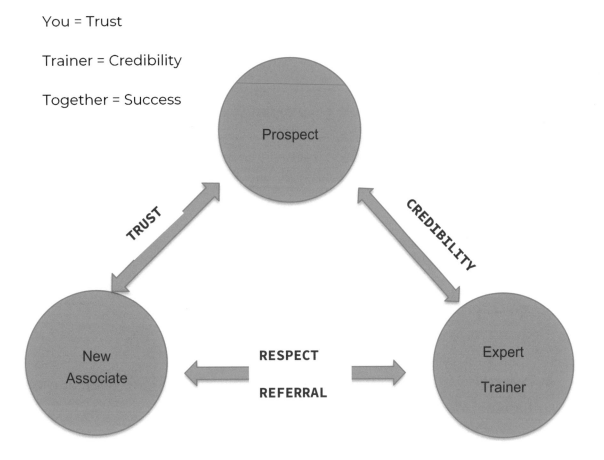

Tip: Some friends and family may not want you to know their personal financial and health affairs. Serve them by introducing them to your Director and/or trainer who will be able to properly serve them and meet their needs.

KEY POINTS TO REMEMBER IN MAKING CONTACT

- **Show enthusiasm and passion for FinFit Life**. Be proud of FinFit Life and your association with the company. Remember, we are offering important services that can truly make a difference for many families. Everyone wants more wealth and health.
- **Keep the invite clear and concise**. DO NOT START answering questions; invite your guest to see the full picture at the presentation. Our goal is not to "give" the presentation at this point, but rather to "get" them to see the presentation and experience our culture. This is an invitation NOT a presentation.
- **Build upon a good rapport and relationship with them**. We always strive to strengthen the relationship of the prospect and associate of FinFit Life.
- **Encourage both the prospect and their spouse to see the presentation**. Have them experience the FinFit Life story together. This will help them make a more committed decision as a family on whether to get involved or become a client.
- **Master the invitation**. Key is to effectively communicate why they would want to learn about who we are and what we do.

RULES OF THUMB FOR MAKING PHONE CALLS

- Stand up when making phone calls. (Motion creates emotion)
- The number 1 reason for making a phone call is to set an appointment.
- Phone call should always be 2 minutes or less.
- Make an invitation, not give a presentation, or justify why they should meet with us.
- Always start with a compliment and how you are looking forward to meeting with them.
- Assume that they are going to meet with you.
- Never ask for their time, take their time.
- If you have to leave a message, always mention that it is a time sensitive matter. "Please call me back ASAP. Today preferably."

Goal: 3-10 successful joint invites with your leadership provides the confidence and skill for the new associate to market the opportunity of FinFit Life independently.

THE OPPORTUNITY

When beginning to explain the opportunity that FinFit Life offers to a prospect, there are a few key points you should communicate.

1. FinFit Life is dedicated to educating all people on how to create and have more wealth and health with the lifestyle to enjoy it.

2. FinFit Life is the first of its kind, revolutionizing both the financial services industry and health industry by helping entrepreneurs start a business that can help change people's futures. We are truly making a difference in the communities we serve.

PART ONE

- Present the fundamental goodness of FinFit Life – how we treat each, other and what we do for the consumer. Appeal to the noble side of their character.
  - Convey directly to the prospect:
    - FinFit Life treats its clients and Associates right.
    - FinFit Life Associates are appreciated and recognized for what they do each day to help and serve people.
    - FinFit Life is committed to helping people and it is rewarding to make a difference in people's lives.
    - FinFit Life Associates teach people what they need to do to manage their own financial futures and how to create true wealth and security and good health to live the lifestyle they deserve and desire. We believe in what we do, we know it's right and we know that we can help and serve people.

PART TWO

- Illustrate what is in it for the prospect.
- Watch for the prospect's reactions to certain issues. A prospect's body language and facial expressions usually tell you what issues interest them the most, and you can zero in on them.

- Some issues you can discuss:
  - The ability to build your own business and be in control of your time, income and happiness.
  - The chance to generate a substantial income, get out of debt and have true peace of mind of future financial independence and security.
  - The opportunity to do things for your family that, until now, you were unable to do.
- Enthusiastically strive to get the prospect fired up about the possibility of a better quality of life than they have now.
- Communicate and share your personal testimony of how you feel about your own future with FinFit Life.
- Be sincere, upbeat and excited.

INVITATION TO YOUR WARM MARKET

Once you are no longer in training, you will want to invite people to a CORPORATE OVERVIEW or One-on-one presentation without your field trainer. Following are suggested steps you can use for the invitation. As always, remember to keep a positive attitude and personalize the invitation.

Remember to smile before you make any calls!

1. **Market the opportunity. Express what excites you**.
   Share with the prospect the reason why you became passionate about FinFit Life and what it has meant to you. When people hear about your goals and excitement, it should spark interest in the opportunity.

2. **Get Their Attention. You are serious, are they?**
   Determine whether the prospect is open to a new possibility.
   "But_____, I've never really talked to you much about these kinds of things. Would any of these things be important to you?" [Wait for Answer e.g. "Sure, but what is it?]

   "_____, before I take any more of my time or yours, I want to ask you a question. If I were to talk to you about a serious legitimate business opportunity, would you listen?"

3. **Briefly explain FinFit Life.**

Share with the prospect our companies name and mission:

"Our company is called FinFit Life and it is all in the name. We are helping people become financially fit, physically fit so that they can have great wealth and health with the lifestyle to enjoy it. It is a revolutionary and first of its kind firm with tremendous income potential for all. But I'm not going to try to explain it all to you now for a couple of reasons:"

- "I've just gotten started, and I don't know how to explain it all. You need to hear it from an expert."
- "It takes about 45 minutes to give you a complete overview, and I don't have the time right now."
- There are some things you have to see visually for it to make sense, and we obviously can't do it over the phone."

"However, my director is giving a special overview on _____ or _____. Which times would be better for you?"

Remember, this is the invitation and not the time to start answering questions or trying to complete the presentation. Use curiosity to your favor. It is like movie trailer. No spoiler alerts.

4. **Extend the invitation.**

The CORPORATE OVERVIEW or one-on-one meeting will allow the prospect to see exactly what they want to know in the most effective way.

Tell the prospect that the meeting will allow him/her to :

"Learn exactly who we are, what we do and how we get paid, which is what most people want to know anyway."

5. **Get a commitment.**

Once you determine what day and time would be best for them, nail down the date and ask them to make sure not to forget or try not to reschedule as it is important to you.

6. **Put them at Ease**. No decisions will be asked for at the introduction. Let the prospect know the purpose of the meeting is to simply provide an introduction to our mission, cause and purpose of FinFit Life and what the benefits are for others. Also, if they want to look at if further then there will be further information provided for them and in no way will there be any pressure to decide on anything.

7. **Overcome Objections**.

   Occasionally, in the course of the invitation, the prospect may begin to ask questions such as:

   > "What is it?"
   > "What are you selling?"
   > "Can you tell me more right now?"

   Remind the prospect that you mentioned you will not be trying to explain it all over the phone for reasons stated and that the whole purpose of meeting is to answer all the questions of who, what and why. Stay positive and excited. Reassure them that in the worst case, you want their feedback and opinion as you value their response.

"Well_____, as I told you, I am really not the one to explain this to you, and it does take more time than I have right now to do it justice. Although when I asked you if you would be willing just to listen, were you telling me the truth?"

EFFECTIVE WAYS TO HANDLE OBJECTIONS

- To keep the positive momentum of the invitation, you should have a few responses in mind.
- Have an objection response "script" in mind. See your trainer for proven effective script manual.
- Familiarize yourself with the most common objections people give you. There are only about 5-10 objections you will ever have to overcome.
- Never answer a question with a statement, answer it with another question.
- Listen twice as much as you talk.
- Strive to be more interested in the other person as opposed to getting them interested in you.
- Be more certain about your proposal than the other person is about objecting.
- Respond honestly and accurately. If you don't know the answer, write down the question and get back to them with a correct answer.

Remember:

- Just because someone has been contacted and may decline does not mean you should never contact them again about the opportunity. It stands to reason the more times you make contact, the more they'll learn about FinFit Life, and the greater the likelihood he/she will say yes to your invitation. Many times, it is just timing.
- **Avoid the Scenario of Disaster.** If you start answering too many questions, it takes the edge off the prospect's curiosity. Do not give it away, take it away.
- You do not have to talk to prospects alone. Your leader will help you.
- You do not have to make a presentation. Your leader or trainer provides the presentation.
- You do not have to answer questions from a prospect. Your leader will field them for you.

Once again, sometimes the timing for a prospect to join FinFit Life or to become a client is not right. We find it takes 5-6 "touches" to provoke a person's interest. The key is to cultivate the relationship respectfully. Conduct a personalized drip campaign over several weeks or months, without sending messages too frequently or coming across as overbearing.

Be sure to practice the scripts repeatedly on the phone with your leader, with someone in your family, or with a friend. You will want to ensure that you are comfortable with the scripts and overcoming possible objections that may arise.

FinFit Life has several effective, proven Phone Scripts that will be of great help to you in building your business. We encourage you to practice these scripts repeatedly until you feel comfortable, so you conduct effective phone calls with confidence.

Social Media **Approach**

We covered the power of using social media to reconnect with people and to meet new people in Step 2: Prospecting. It is also important to follow social media etiquette during contact as well. Make sure to follow FinFit Life on all channels for great shareable content and find the latest trends at learn.finfitlife.com.

Using social media sites like Facebook, Instagram, Twitter, and LinkedIn, can be used to contact people just as you would in real life. Often, it has been some time since you have seen many of the friends you reach out to on social media. Your first contact with them should not be business-related, but should be something like this:

> "_____ (Their Name), It has been a long time. I hope life has been treating you well. What are you up to these days?"

This is the type of message that you would expect from a friend. It does not seem as if you contacted them just to talk business. They will usually respond by updating you on their life and then they will ask about yours.

Sample Response:

> *"Glad to hear things are going well for you. I just got started with an exciting new company that is giving me a chance to make some serious extra income helping others learn a few simple techniques so that they can build true financial independence for their family. If you would like, I could message or text you some information so you can see exactly what we are doing and how it works."*

They may respond with their mobile number. Then, follow the steps of the Video Contact from earlier in this chapter to make contact.

On business-oriented social media sites like LinkedIn, it is acceptable to network and extends business opportunities to people. Use the same scripts from the Video Contact that we covered earlier in the chapter. Be up-front with them and do not try to make FinFit Life appear like a salaried position.

Our opportunity stands strong on its own and is very attractive to entrepreneurial people from all business backgrounds, whether they are looking for a career change or just a second income. Be sure to make social media a part of building your FinFit Life business. Use social media the right way and extend the same courtesies you would like extended to you.

Indirect Social Media Contact

Another way to grow your business through social media is to share the posts from the FinFit Life social media sites on your page.

FinFit Life's social media feeds that include many useful posts that you can share with your friends and followers. Just go to your social media sites, search for the FinFit Life pages, click "like" or "follow" and you will start receiving the feeds. When you see posts you like, simply click "like" and then "share" to post the content on your page with your comments.

Your friends will see inspirational or entertaining posts and become curious about what you are doing. After doing this consistently, many Associates have been contacted by friends who want to know more about the company.

This is another great way to expose the opportunity to people you have connected with on social media. Get in the habit of "liking" and "sharing" the company's posts to help grow your business.

Drill for Skill on the Contact

- 90% of failure in this business takes place during the contact.

- There are two simple reasons why most people fail in the approach – doing it wrong or simply not doing it.

The key to overcoming these two problems is to train every Associate to become a "Master Inviter." You would not want new Associates to practice with the people on their prospect list and make a bad first impression. You must give every new associate some intense simulated training to prepare them for the real thing.

Simulated Contact Training

The key to quality contact is to hold training sessions with your leaders that "simulate" real contact. This can be done for both the Conference Call Follow-Up and the Phone Invitation Script.

The best way to do this is by getting at least three Associates on the phone with each taking turns as the leader, the new Associate, and the prospect. Take it easy on each other at first, until everyone gets comfortable with the scripts and the flow. Then, instruct the Associate playing the prospect to get tougher and more skeptical, asking questions that are more difficult. You can even practice text messaging sessions with each other using the same methods.

This type of training will help both the leader and the new Associate learn how to overcome almost any objection. It will not only give your new and old leaders the knowledge and experience to make quality invitations, but it will also give them the confidence to approach even more prospects.

Step 3: Contact Conclusion

The leaders with the highest/ or highest number of quality contacts build the biggest teams, which leads to a larger client base, which leads to more success and income for you and your leaders. Make sure they understand that enthusiasm and understanding human nature are key. Always train, train, train on the Contact.

We challenge you to personally contact a minimum of 10-25 people, per week, to see a presentation whether in a One-on-One, Group, or Online setting. If you are part-time with FinFit Life, aim for 5-10 people.

The future belongs to those who believe in the beauty of their dreams.

— Eleanor Roosevelt

STEP 4 PRESENTATION

Purpose: To present the power of the FinFit Life story to your prospects.

Now that we have made our prospect list and contacted the prospects, it is time to tell them the FinFit Life story by way of a Corporate Overview. Don't forget to visit learn.finfitlife.com for the latest version of the Corporate Overview and to watch a recording of a recent one.

There are three types of Corporate Overviews at FinFit Life:

Group Corporate Overview

These meetings take place in hotels or offices in front of a live crowd. They are effective because the prospect sees the story in-person, and feels the energy of the crowd.

Online Corporate Overview

Online presentations, webinars, videos, etc. are meetings that take place online. They are live or pre-recorded using services like Zoom, AnyMeeting, Teams, or other platforms. With online Corporate Overviews, it is easy to capture all your guest's contact information which simplifies your follow-up!

One-On-One Corporate Overview

These meetings take place in the home or office of the prospect usually with a new Associate and their leader.

All of these types of presentations are highly effective. You can use any of them to help build your FinFit Life business.

Corporate Overview Basics

No matter which format you choose, the presentation must be compelling, powerful, and conducted by your most enthusiastic leaders.

Even if you are not the greatest speaker, keep in mind that people respond to presenters who are genuine and passionate about what they do. Those are the most important characteristics of an effective presentation.

Newer leaders should always let an experienced leader share the story on their behalf. Do not tell the story to your prospect until you have had experience. The leader will also move the prospect to the next step as well.

What a Successful Corporate Overview Expresses

- There is a huge need for what we do; people need to save money and want to make more money.
- We are good people doing good things to help other people.
- FinFit Life is financially rewarding.
- People from all walks of life have become successful with FinFit Life, and you have the same potential for success.

Keys to a Successful Corporate Overview

- Keep the meeting simple.
- Use the company-approved business presentation.
- Use a conversational speaking style and an easy, pleasant delivery.
- Let your presentation come from the heart.
- Market the potential of the business opportunity, but do not overhype it.
- Keep an exciting, fun pace.
- Make people feel special. Make the extra effort to call people by their names from the stage so they feel as if they are part of the meeting.
- Use FinFit Life confirmation list to tract and confirm prospects that have responded positively to the invitation.
- Study audio and video recordings of other leaders giving the presentation.
- Always present a strong focus on our consumer value proposition.

When presenting, make sure each prospect feels the tremendous conviction and enthusiasm you have for FinFit Life and this great opportunity. Imagine each prospect in your audience becoming a successful leader, and how that could change their family's financial future.

The Group Corporate Overview

The Group Presentation takes place in hotels or offices in front of a live crowd.

Group Corporate Overview s are very effective, as prospects hear the story live, feeling both the energy of the crowd and the sincerity of the speaker. The more people who attend a group Corporate Overview, the more excitement the meeting will generate.

Pre-Meeting Preparation

It is important to be totally prepared for every Group Corporate Overview s. Every aspect of your presentation—body language, tone, delivery— should contribute to an exciting, yet professional environment. The appropriate environment will help guests feel good about becoming part of FinFit Life.

Meeting Roles

- **Introducer** — Introduces the presenter who is running the corporate overview for the guests.
- **Presenter** — Presents the corporate overview.
- **Testimonial** — Current associate that can share their experience with FinFit Life and share a little bit of how they came to FinFit Life.

Meeting Room Logistics

Prepare the room by setting up your equipment (computer, projector, screen, etc.) in advance and setting a comfortable temperature. Play upbeat music before the meeting to help set the tone. Prepare the sign-in sheets and any other handouts well in advance. Have hot or cold drinks (no alcohol) prepared to create an appropriate environment for socializing.

FINFIT
LIFE

Confirmation List

My Name:	My Director:
Date Completed:	Director Review:

	First Name	Last Name	Phone Number	Email	Associate	Invited By
1						
2						
3						
4						
5						
6						
7						
8						
9						
10						
11						
12						
13						
14						
15						

Leaders should finish the logistics 45 minutes before the meeting, allowing for plenty of time to greet their fellow leaders and guests as they arrive. Guests should arrive 30 minutes early to meet the speakers and leaders, and to help alleviate any skepticism they may have.

Building a rapport with the new guests is essential to breaking the ice and making them feel comfortable. Encourage the presenters to meet as many guests as possible before the meeting starts.

Mental Preparation

Prepare yourself mentally before the meeting. Your enthusiasm and passion need to be conveyed during your presentation. Leave all negativity at the door.

Appearance

Wearing appropriate attire is very important. This is a business meeting, whether you are speaking or not.

Pre-Corporate Overview Activities

When you arrive, go directly into the meeting room and introduce yourself to all attendees, creating a warm, welcoming environment. Do not wait in the hallways or lobby. Keep your conversations positive and upbeat.

Have everyone sign in and take a nametag. Use one color nametag for FinFit Life Associates and another for new guests. Write the first names large on the tag so that the speakers can call people by their name from the stage. Introduce your guests to your leaders and to the presenter, and then find a seat for your guests near the front of the room.

During the Meeting

Show the current, approved FinFit Life Corporate Overview presentation and any recruiting videos on a computer (through a projector).

If you are not the speaker, do not Associates or answer any questions the speaker asks the crowd during the meeting. Give the new guests a chance to answer so they can become part of the meeting. Try not to get up and leave during the meeting, and even if it is your thousandth meeting, look interested and take notes. Following these guidelines will help the new guests recognize the importance of the meeting and give energy to the speaker.

The Meeting Close

The presenter will close the meeting by issuing a challenge to the new guests, beginning the follow-up process.

The presenter will say something like:

> *"Thank you for coming out tonight. If you are excited about exploring the FinFit Life opportunity further or simply just want to have your current plan reviewed for free, we ask you to please connect with the person who invited you here and set up a time to meet with their leader within the next 24-48 hours.*

> *Why in the next 24-48 hours? Well, we have found it is always better to meet when your impressions of what you saw today are still fresh in your mind. Plus, our most successful leaders are usually the ones who get off to a fast start. So please make sure to set an appointment before you leave, and we will get you started on the right track. Thank you for coming out tonight. We will be around for a while to answer any questions you may have. Again, thank you."*

This conclusion will be the perfect set-up for Step 5: Follow-Up.

It is important to devote time immediately after the meeting to setting appointments and answering questions from new guests. Once all the guests' needs are satisfied, business or leader meetings can be conducted.

The Online Corporate Overview

The Online Presentation is one of the best ways to spread the FinFit Life story to people in multiple locations or those who cannot attend a live meeting.

In today's fast-paced world, some people struggle to find the time to attend a meeting or host someone in their home. The online presentation, or webinar, is a perfect solution for them.

Run your Online Presentations on a regularly scheduled basis 2-3 times a week, and be prepared to conduct impromptu One-on-One Online Presentations as needed throughout the week. You can also use the approved recorded Corporate Overview that streams 24/7 to fit every schedule.

Be sure to set up your Online Corporate Overview with a registration page so you can capture key information from your guests. This will make the follow-up an easier process.

Live Online Meeting Presentation Preparation

Online presentations can be done from anywhere— if you have access to a computer, high-speed internet connectivity, and software like Zoom, Google Hangouts, AnyMeeting, WebEx, MS Teams, or other services.

Materials and Room

Be sure to use the current, approved FinFit Life Corporate Overview, and reserve a quiet room where you will not be disturbed.

Mental Preparation

Be mentally prepared before starting. You must convey your enthusiasm and passion for what FinFit Life can do for your guests during your presentation. Eliminate any negative thoughts from your mind.

The Online Corporate Overview Close

The presenter will conclude the meeting by issuing the same challenge to the new guests as they would during the Group Meetings, with just a few small changes to the wording.

The presenter will say something like:

> *"Thank you for joining us tonight. If you are excited about exploring the FinFit Life opportunity further or simply just want to have your current plan reviewed for free, connect with the person who invited you to this presentation and set up an appointment with his/her leader within the next 24 to 48 hours.*
>
> *Why in the next 24 to 48 hours? Well, we have found it is always better to meet when your thoughts and impressions of what you saw today are still fresh in your mind. Plus, our most successful leaders are usually the ones that get off to a fast start. So please, make sure you set up an appointment as soon as we log off to get you started on the right track.*
>
> *Thanks for taking the time to listen tonight. I look forward to meeting you personally at the next FinFit Life event. Thank you again."*

One-on-One Corporate Overview

If you cannot get the prospect to a live Group or Online Corporate Overview, you can schedule a One-on-One Corporate Overview at the prospect's home or office, or at a restaurant.

One-on-One Corporate Overview Preparation

It is important to prepare for every One-on-One Corporate Overview exactly as you would for a Group or Online Corporate Overview. Remember, every action you take during the presentation contributes to how the guests perceive you and FinFit Life.

Mental Preparation

Prepare yourself mentally before you arrive. You must convey your enthusiasm and passion for what FinFit Life can do for them during your presentation. Leave any of your negative thoughts outside their home.

Appearance

Proper attire is very important. You should be dressed in business attire or sharp business casual.

Build Rapport

Take time before you start the presentation to build rapport with them so that they will be more comfortable with you, and so you can know more about them and their family. Try to get both the recruit and their significant other (if they have one) to sit down with you for the presentation.

The One-on-One Corporate Overview

Show the current FinFit Life presentation and any recruiting videos you would like on a notebook computer or tablet. Try to engage the prospect and their significant other with questions throughout the presentation. Make sure that they feel your conviction and enthusiasm for the FinFit Life opportunity.

If you accompany the presenter but are not presenting, remember to appear very interested and allow the presentation to flow. Remain silent but engaged unless the presenter asks you to comment.

One-on-One Corporate Overview Close

If the prospect wants to join immediately, sign them up and then set a date for their Fast Start Interview. If the prospect decides not to join, still fill out the Needs Analysis data form. Then analyze their current plan and set an appointment to review the results. Remember to also ask for referrals of anyone they know who would like to save money or make extra money.

One-on-One Corporate Overviews are a great tool to help build your business. You are able to see families in their homes or sit down for breakfast and lunch meetings near your prospects' places of employment.

Focus on Corporate Overview Results

As a business leader, you must monitor all activities within your organization. This includes the Corporate Overview whether it is shown in a Group setting, One-on-One or Online.

Develop projections for each Corporate Overview and evaluate how your team did. Use the sign-in log and determine the status of each new guest:

- Was the proper follow-up conducted?
- Did guests receive an email or text message following the event?
- Did any guests who agreed to a follow-up interview not show up?
- Were they contacted to find out why?

Examine every aspect surrounding your Corporate Overview flow to detect and fix any breakdowns in the system. Share your findings with your team in a constructive, respectful way.

Everyone on the team has a stake in the success of the meeting. Work together to find solutions that ensure a positive outcome for future Corporate Overviews.

Step 4: Presentation Conclusion

The leaders with the most qualified prospects at exciting, professional Corporate Overviews will have the most success.

Our challenge to you is to host a minimum of two Group CORPORATE OVERVIEWs, and two live Online Corporate Overviews per week. Fill in the rest with One-on-One Corporate Overviews so that your system is running at full speed and with full coverage by your team members.

I have no special talent. I am only passionately curious.

— Albert Einstein

STEP 5 FOLLOW-UP

Purpose: To position the prospect to sign up with FinFit Life and/or become a client.

The Importance of the **Follow-Up**

The follow-up to the presentation is as equally critical as establishing the initial contact. The main focus of the follow-up is always to help the prospect to decide to join FinFit Life as an Associate, or to become a client.

When the follow-up is properly executed, you will recruit a higher percentage of prospects. As a byproduct of the system, you will also bring in a greater number of clients.

You may need to follow up several times. This is typical and it is considered a best practice. Some of your largest sales and successes may come after 7 follow-ups and after the client said no previously.

Drill for Skill Training

Always conduct Drill for Skill training sessions on carrying out successful Follow-up Interviews. Simulate real contact with prospects, just like your preparations for the Contact stage. These focused training sessions give your leaders the confidence to know what to say and to say it each and every time.

Master the Follow-Up for Success

Ensure that you and your leaders master the art of the follow-up to maximize the results from all Corporate Overviews. The follow-up step varies depending on which presentation type you choose, but one thing never changes: You must follow the same process for every meeting.

One-on-One Corporate Overview Follow-Up

When the One-on-One Corporate Overview ends, it is time to move your prospect into to the Associate decision phase and schedule their follow-up appointment. If the prospect wants to join immediately, sign them up on the spot, and set a date for their Fast Start Interview.

If they decide not to join, try to bring them to a group Corporate Overview or at least try to make them a client. Remember to ask for referrals of anyone they know who would like to realize the dream of financial independence.

Sample Referral Script:

> *"As you can tell, these concepts will have a dramatic impact on your financial future. The amazing part is that most people have never even heard of FinFit Life. Who in your life would benefit from at least hearing our story, so they can have the same opportunity that you did to learn what FinFit Life can do for them?"*

Group Corporate Overview Follow-Up

As soon as the Group Corporate Overview ends, the follow-up begins. As outlined in Step 4, the presenter issued a challenge to the new guests: meet with the person who invited them and schedule a Fast Start Interview with their leader within the next 24-48 hours.

Saying the wrong thing after the meeting ends can dramatically affect your results. One tendency is to say something like "So, what did you think?" This response puts the new guest in the power position, and you lose control of the follow-up. It opens the door for a guest to revert to the human nature tendencies of procrastination and excuses. Instead, follow this time-tested script below.

Sample Script:

> *"Wasn't that great? Let's get with _____ [your leader] to set your appointment."*

If they say "OK" or "Yes", take them to your leader and say:

> *"_____ [Leader], this is _____ [Guest's name]. I wanted you two to meet so we can set a time for their return appointment."*

If they say "No" or "I am not interested", say:

> *"No problem, but I promised _____ [leader] that we would say goodbye before we left."*

Then take them to your leader and say:

> *"_____ [Leader], this is _____ [Guest's name]. We wanted to say goodbye before we left."*

This indicates to the leader that the inviter needs help; the prospect did not want to set an appointment and does not seem interested. The leader then takes over, shakes the guest's hand and in a polite, but assertive manner says:

> *"_____ [Guest's name] it was great having you out tonight. Is tomorrow or the following day better for us to get together so we can take the next step?*

If the guest gives the leader a time, set the appointment immediately. If the guest hesitates, the leader then has a chance to address any concerns or objections, and to provide any answers that could potentially convince the guest to join. At the very least, the leader can help the inviter set up an appointment for a Needs Analysis.

If a new guest stays, sets up an appointment with the leader, and keeps that appointment— you know you have a serious recruit. If a guest leaves quickly or does not set up an appointment, do not waste your time recruiting further. Either the timing was not right or the opportunity was not right for them. Move on to the next person on your prospect list.

Online Presentation Follow-Up

As soon as you log off from the Online Presentation, you should begin calling your guests. If you are the host of the Corporate Overview, download your registration/attendee report and start calling.

They will be expecting a call since the presenter issued a challenge to the new guests at the end of the meeting to set up a Follow-Up appointment within 24 to 48 hours.

Just like the Group Presentation, when you call your guests, resist the tendency to say something like "So, what did you think?" This question puts the guest in the power position; you lose control of the Follow-Up. It opens the door for guests to revert to their natural tendencies to procrastinate or make excuses. Instead, follow this time-tested script below.

Sample Script:

Call the new guest and say:

> *"Hi, _____ [Guest's name]. Wasn't that great! Let's get you on the phone with _____ [your leader] to set your appointment."*

If they say "OK" or "Yes," immediately tie them in with your leader on a 3-way call and say:

> *"Hi, _____ [leader], I have _____ [Guest's name] here on the phone with me now and I wanted you two to meet so we can set a time for their follow-up appointment."*

If they say "No" or make an excuse, say without hesitation:

> *"No problem, but I promised _____ [leader], that I would introduce you two when the presentation ended. Let me connect him/her in with us. Hold on one second."*

Then tie in your leader on a 3-way call and say:

> *"Hi _____ [leader], I have _____ [Guest's name] here on the phone with me now and, as I promised, I wanted to make sure you two met."*

This is the sign to the leader that the inviter needs help – the prospect did not want to set an appointment and does not seem interested.

The leader then takes over and says:

> *"_____ [Guest's name] it was great having you on the webinar tonight. Is tomorrow or the following day better for us to get together so we can take the next step?"*

If the guest gives the leader a time, set up the appointment. If they hesitate this gives the leader a chance to address concerns, clear up objections, and answer questions. The leader may still be able to recruit the guest to FinFit Life.

At the very least, if the prospect decides they do not want to join FinFit Life, the leader can help the inviter sign up the guest for a Needs Analysis and possibly establish a new client.

If a new guest sounds excited, sets up an appointment with the leader, and keeps that appointment— you know you have a serious recruit. If they do not wish to set up the appointment, do not waste your time recruiting further. Either the timing was not right or the opportunity was not right for them to move on to the next person on your prospect list and consider following up with them at a later date.

Step 5: Follow-Up Conclusion

Our challenge to you is mastering the Follow-Up to maximize your results in all areas. Inspire strong commitments and set the direction for each new Associate. If the prospect does not join, be sure to help their family with a free Needs Analysis, providing them better plan for the future.

Two roads diverged in a wood, and I took the one less traveled by, and that has made all the difference.

– Robert Frost

STEP 6 FAST START

Purpose: To get the new associate off to a fast start!

The Importance of the Fast Start

The first few days of a new associate's career with FinFit Life are among the most important moments in their career. That is because, as history has shown us, the faster they start, the better chance they have to succeed.

However, after a prospect has signed up with FinFit Life, your work is far from finished. Now, your responsibility as a leader is to prepare your new associate for any potential obstacles ahead so that they can achieve positive results as soon as possible. Your work is not complete until the new associate becomes a self-sustaining, self-replicating leader at FinFit Life.

Whether a prospect decides to join FinFit Life or not, you should always give your support to everyone you can. Just by providing them with a free Needs Analysis, you are helping that person get their finances off to a Fast Start while creating a better plan for their future. In this way, you are fulfilling the FinFit Life mission by helping as many people as possible to meet their planning needs.

Building their Team

- - - - - - - - - - - - - - -

While all the components of the Fast Start are very important, nothing is more critical than helping your associate build their team quickly out of the gate.

The Fast Start Interview

Starting a new teammate off on the right foot is very important. The Fast Start Interview is the best way to get a firm commitment from the new associate while getting them off to a fast start.

Always spend a few minutes getting to know the new prospect. Make sure the Fast Start Interview is conducted at the office or at another quiet location during the day. The interview can also be conducted online through a Web conferencing service. When possible, the recruiter should plan to attend.

The Fast Start Interview

1. *What intrigued you the most about what you saw in the CORPORATE OVERVIEW (or in the video)? (Listen to their response to identify their area of interest.)*

2. *How do you feel about The FinFit Life Movement and the mission of helping individuals and families pursue better health and wealth?*

3. *Tell me a little about yourself...*

4. *How do you feel about the success you have had in your life up until now?*

5. *What are some of your short and long term goals?*

6. If you were to work with FinFit Life, why would you do it?

7. Do you have any specific questions about any particular aspect of the company or business?

8. Can you think of any reason for not getting started with FinFit Life?

9. *"Now, I have one very important question to ask you: Do you want strong leadership or weak leadership from me?"* (Everyone will, of course, say strong.)

Then say:

"Great. I am glad you said that because a weak leader is someone who wouldn't give you any direction and would just hope you'd figure it out on your own. But a strong leader is someone who will walk you through each step and leaves nothing to chance. "That is what you want right?" They will, of course, say "Yes."

10. "Great! Then there are four things we need to do right away to get you started:

First, we need to get you signed up with FinFit Life. We will do this in just a few minutes.

Second, we will start your Prospect List today. Our goal will be to come up with your initial 100 prospects, and then we will work on narrowing that list down to your Top 25 prospects.

Third, we will work together to identify those prospects who we need to reach out to. After that, we will create an outreach plan and goals to start building your business.

And finally, we are going to have you complete your complimentary Needs Analysis. We do this because it is important for you to understand what we do for people and what we can do for your family as well.

While you are not required to become a client, we believe it makes sense for our Associates to have a sound financial plan in place as well. Do not you agree?

If the prospect gives you any pushback on any of these items just say:

"Well when I asked you if you wanted strong or weak leadership from me and you said strong, were you serious or not?"

They will usually answer that they were serious. Then say:

"Well then let's get _____ (the item that gave you push back on) handled today. Fair enough?"

The Fast Start Outline

1. Give them the link to the FinFit Life website, sign him/her with FinFit Life, and have them pay the fee.

2. Use the Memory Jogger Sheet to at least create his/her Top 25 Prospect List, if the conversation is going well and you have the time, try and get his/her initial 100 names.

3. Introduce them to the Team Builder Program, which will put them in the best position for success.

   You say:

   "As we get started, I want you to know that with FinFit Life, you are in business for yourself, but not by yourself. We are building your "company" (or team) within a company, FinFit Life. Therefore, of all the people on this list, who are the 12 people that you have always wanted to be in business with and would want to have on your "Board of Directors?" (Mark the ones they select.)

   Then say:

   "Great, our goal then is to get at least five to six of these people in business with you over the next two to three weeks."

   They will, of course, say "Yes". Then say:

   "Since we are going to be contacting these prospects, you probably want to know how we can help them, right?"

   "We are going to do the exact same thing for those prospects and the people they bring on board because they are all building their own company within a company as well. Can you see how big your team can get in a fairly short period of time?"

   (We will discuss the Team Builder Program in more detail later in this chapter.

4. Schedule a meeting to help them establish contact with their prospects using Step 3 - The Contact.

5. Go over the FinFit Life Field Training Program Agreement and explain how the program and reimbursement works.

6. Walk them through the Business Blueprint if you have not done so already. During this step, you will help them identify their core values, which will determine their path, pace, and the sacrifices needed to achieve their Family, Business, and Individual goals.

Use the Fast Start Interview with each prospect who attends a presentation. It will help your new associate firm up their commitment and get started on doing the things that will put you and them in the best position to succeed right away.

Field Training

Field Training is the initial direction you give to the new Associate so that they can learn the ropes of the business. Every new associate should immediately sign up with a Field Trainer in order to get off to a Fast Start.

The Field Trainer is responsible for training the new associate in:

*   Prospecting
*   Contacting
*   How to conduct a solid three-way follow-up
*   How to give a great sales presentation
*   How to do a Fast Start Interview

Don't forget to visit learn.finfitlife.com for a digital copy of the fast start documents!

The Focus of Proper Field Training

Most people who see the FinFit Life story are intrigued by the idea of leveraging their time to build a team of their own. They expect that their efforts will be focused on this proposition. However, some leaders in this industry have a tendency to start by having their new Associate focus on getting licensed and making sales instead. We call this the "Scenario of a Slow Start."

The "Scenario of a Slow Start"

- Sign up the new associate
- Focus on getting licensed ASAP
- Train him/her in all the technicalities so he/she can market FinFit-approved products and services.

Alternatively, we can use...

The "Scenario of a Fast Start"

- Sign up the new associate
- Surround him/herself with people
- Surround his/her people with more people

In the "Scenario of a Slow Start", we have a new associate who was excited about the possibility of building a team when they saw the presentation, but then was trained by their leader on the technicalities of marketing only the products and services we offer. As soon as they have a bad day, or have a person quit, you will probably never see that associate again.

In the "Scenario of a Fast Start," we have a new associate whose leader helped them build a team. When they have a bad day or have a person quit, they are not going anywhere because they have a team in place. By focusing on building a team you have, "locked them in" to the business and you are putting them in the best position to succeed.

One of the most important features of the fast start is the Top 25 list. Just as your Top 25 list helped you fast start, the Top 25 lists of the people you recruit are going to provide your team an opportunity to multiply. Also, this will be the key step in surrounding him/her with people, and then surrounding his/her people with more people.

Top 25 Lists Chart

Business Builders	Top 25 List	Top 12 People you want to work with	Families Helped	Associates	Key Component
You	25 close contacts	12 potential Associates	3 families	3 business builders	Surrounding yourself with people
3 Associates	75 close contacts	36 potential Associates	9 families	9 business builders	Surrounding your people with people
12 Associates	300 close contacts	144 potential Associates	36 families	36 business builders	Your baseshop is built
48 Associates	1200 close contacts	576 potential Associates	144 families	144 business builders	

Will they still learn how to market the product?

Absolutely, but we will not hold them back from building a team until they become experts. From Day One, Associates will have joint appointments with their leader while building their team. They will learn and become experts by observing the many client presentations that their leaders present to new Associates and business prospects. They will also develop their skills through quality field training from field trainers within their Base Shop.

Will they still get licensed?

Yes! Our standard is that all new Financial Fitness Associates be licensed within 30 days of joining our team. This way, the new associate can receive a commission when the team they built and trained starts making sales. Once a FinFit Life FFA gets licensed we have an opportunity with the help of your Director to announce a Grand Opening for your business. This is where you will invite family, friends, coworkers, etc. to learn about your business and celebrate you. We have many marketing materials that are designed to help you and your Director promote and market your Grand Opening. Check with your Director for more details and they can also be found on learn.finfitlife.com

Will they miss meetings or even worse, quit?

Not likely. They see that if they do quit, they have more to lose because they would let down the team they have in place. Very often, the fear of loss motivates people more than the hope for gain.

The Power of the Team Builder Program Training

The key is to help EVERY associate get at least five direct Associates within the first two to three weeks. That way, if your Associates decide to leave the business for whatever reason, you have protected your time investment, because you now have leaders who will report directly to you.

Use the Team Builder Script, which is found in the Fast Start Interview, every time, and you will be on the way to experiencing exponential growth within your team.

Imagine the results as your recruit gets five of their own Associates in the first few weeks. Then he/she continues the program, helping each team member to recruit five more Associates.

5 x 5 = 25, then continue the process...

25 x 5 = 125

125 x 5 = 625

It does not take long for exponential growth to take over, meaning the new associate can build a large organization quickly. Even if people fall a little short and only get three to four new Associates in their first two to three weeks, these numbers are progress and worth celebrating.

Within the first 30 days, you should perform field training with the new associate to achieve the following results:

- Use the Team Builder Program to recruit 5 to 10 new Associates in the first few weeks.
- Perform a minimum of 5 Needs Analyses/onboard new clients.
- Complete Field Training for three to four nights per week and weekends, if they choose, with the goal of delivering at least 10 presentations a week.

The FinFit Life **Four Step** Sales Process

Whether someone joins FinFit Life or chooses to become a client, it is important to use the same sales process each and every time. This ensures that every client has the right plan in place designed to meet his or her individual needs. It also gives your team a consistent model to work with.

There are **Four Important Steps** of every sale-

- **The 1st Step | Introduction:** Give the Corporate Overview or Client Presentation and then complete the Financial Needs Analysis. Be sure to schedule the follow-up appointment using the following script:

    "I am excited to follow-up with you so we can review the results of your needs analysis. How does your schedule look on _____ or _____ (Choose two days within 48-72 hours) to review the recommendations?"

    If they resist, or try and put you off just say:

    "One area I see that you need immediate help in is that you do not have living benefits. We need to get this fixed right away, in case something was to happen and you were not covered. How does your schedule look on _____ (Day of the week) to review the results of your Needs Analysis?"

And/or say:

"One area (or, another area) where I see an opportunity for progress is that your savings are not protected from any sudden market corrections. We need to get this fixed right away to protect your hard-earned money. How is your schedule looking on _____ (Day of the week) to review the results of your Needs Analysis?"

Feel free to make your message more personal by sharing your own stories of people who waited until after it was too late to get covered or protected. Give examples about someone who did take advantage of these concepts and was covered when an incident occurred. You can also use any of the FinFit Life living benefits videos to drive these points home.

The key is to create a sense of urgency, so that the prospect is looking forward to reviewing and implementing a better plan to protect and build wealth for their family.

- **The 2nd Step | Fact Finder:** Review the results, show product-specific presentations, and implement the recommendations by completing the appropriate applications.
- **The 3rd Step | Closing:** Deliver the policy and/or contracts. Be sure to go over the policy or contract with the client. Let them know that you will follow up with them from time to time, and that if they have any questions, to call you anytime.
- **The 4th Step | Follow-Up:** Provide ongoing support and grow engagement through the FinFit Life Fitness challenge and vitality program. This is always a great opportunity to increase the sale and ask for referrals!

Fast Start Conclusion

We challenge you to do whatever it takes to put every new recruit in the best position for success. You can get him or her off to a fast and effective start by using all the techniques in this chapter including: setting high expectations upfront, mastering the Fast Start Interview, surrounding the new Associate with people, and making sure everyone has a Needs Analysis completed. Look at each new leader as a future FinFit Life Legend and help them make their dreams and goals come true.

The two most important days in your life are the day you are born and the day you find out why.

— Mark Twain

STEP 7 DUPLICATION

Purpose: To duplicate and run the system that creates new leaders and production simultaneously. The key to building your team is having field trainers as you grow. Never forget to train the trainer.

Duplication Leads to **Your Ultimate Success**

This Business Building Blueprint:
- Allows you to leverage your time to multiply your efforts and earnings.
- Allows you to spend time doing the work you love to do, rather than the work you have to do.
- Allows for duplication in others so that the thousandth leader is a good as the first.
- Allows you to apply abilities that you can learn and develop, rather than relying on special talents.
- Allows you to work within a model that is system driven, not personality driven.
- Allows you to benefit from a system that is predictable, proven, and profitable.
- Allows you to run the system while the system runs the business.
- Allow you to experience explosive, exponential growth.

To build a business that enables you to achieve your dreams, you must:
- Duplicate yourself and the system with your leaders to build a giant distribution organization.
- Continuously open new "outlets" to build your business.
- Work on your business, not in your business. Work on building a business, not on doing business.
- Build a "prototype" that can be duplicated.

Remember two things:
1. The key is to imitate, not create.
2. Marketing is the opening of outlets and the gathering of clients simultaneously.

Become a Master Duplicator/Replicator

Repeat the FinFit Life Business System Seven Steps repeatedly. The speed and precision with which you copy and execute the system will largely determine your success, and this same precision must be duplicated throughout your team.

The Power of **Duplication**

5 Steps to Turn Yourself into the Perfect Copy Machine

1. Find a plan that works and make sure to apply to every new associate. (The FinFit Life Business System).
2. Repeat it over and over again.
3. The repetition of simple things leads to an inevitable explosion.
4. Develop cookie-cutter exactness.
5. Create a machine that builds and runs your business.

The Key Components of Duplication Include:

- Take on a recruiter's mentality.
- Adopt a builder's mindset.
- Allow enough time for your efforts to compound.
- Do not quit – most people have a survival phase as they get their business up and running.
- Train each Associate to ensure you have duplication throughout your team. Teach them exactly what they need to know to win.
- Keep the information and training simple.
- Create an easy-to-follow, transferable blueprint for your business, motivation, recognition systems and recruiting programs.
- Master the system, and then keep it the same.
- Study the system over and over in every facet of the business.
- Make sure you are the master copy worth duplicating to ensure a high-performance level throughout your team.

Keys to **Exponential Growth**

You Must Build:

- **Wide** – You can never have too many direct leaders.
- **Deep** – Use overlapping leadership to drive the multiples and help your leaders succeed.
- **Service** – Exceptional service to direct clients and downline is a key to exceptional Growth

Two Main Focal Points:

- Get more personal direct Associates.
- Get more prospects and leaders for your CORPORATE OVERVIEWs.

Focus on building a big leadership team and a large client base simultaneously.

Right off the bat, recognize that no matter how good our value proposition is, some people will just not want to join. Do not let that frustrate you. Simply move on to the next new prospect. The scary part is that the ones who are serious and the ones who are not serious all look the same. You simply have to tell the story over and over, putting the law of averages to work for you.

Compress more activity into shorter time for explosive growth.

A successful leader monitors his activity and focuses on results.

A leader **must:**

- Track prospect lists and the number of contacts being made weekly.
- Run leaders' meetings after the Corporate Overviews to monitor the numbers and follow-up.
- Track the number of Fast Start Interviews.
- Track the number of new Associate sign-ups.
- Track the number of Need Analyses completed.
- Help all of your leaders in these areas to stay disciplined and accountable.
- Use the FinFit Life Activity to Results Tracker Sheet for your personal activity. Send this sheet to your leader weekly and have your leaders share their sheets with you on a weekly basis as well. Discipline & Accountability lead to Big-Time Success!
- Use a system of recognition and motivation
- Run a "Hero-making Machine" to recognize and motivate your leaders at all levels. People today are starved for recognition.
- Have a Fast Start Award for new Associates.
- Schedule three to four-day activity blitzes every few weeks.
- Hold activity contests that run every one to two weeks.
- Establish high expectations and standards for your people.
- Share team news.
- Conduct a team leader's bulletin
- Schedule local meetings and special events often.

Avoid the three causes of panic leadership:

- Lack of activity.

- Lack of earnings and savings.

- Lack of a definite system.

Two keys to big-time recruiting:
- Feel good about FinFit Life and what we do for people.

- Then get others (Associates and clients) to feel the same way.

Set an inspirational example. Always:
- Recruit the most.

- Make and save the most money.

- Be the hardest worker.

- Be the most passionate.

- Be the most excited.

- Be the most positive.

- Be the most committed

Keep the Main Thing the Main Thing

How do you know if you are doing this, simply ask yourself these three questions:

- **Question #1** - Do you have your CURRENT Top 25 Prospect List with you at all times?

- **Question #2** - How many contacts/invitations did you make last week and WHO SPECIFICALLY are you going to contact this week?
    - POOR 0-5 contacts a week
    - AVG. 5-10 contacts a week
    - GOOD 10-25 contacts a week
    - GREAT 25+ contacts a week

- **Question #3** - Do YOUR LEADERS have their current Top 25
  - ○ Prospect List, how many contacts did they make last week, and most importantly, who are they going to contact this week?

Once these three main points are focused on, then it is just a matter of:
- Running smooth, exciting presentations.
- Making sure Follow-Up appointments are set.
- Ensuring that Fast Start Interviews are done correctly.
- Having leaders effectively explain the benefits of FinFit Life.
- Making sure new Associates swiftly begin to repeat the process - FinFit Life is a business of duplication!

Use Events to **Maximize Growth**

Leverage Your Local, Regional and National Events

Our business thrives on personal connections and relationships, as well as continuous learning and development. Thus, an effective strategy in building your business is to leverage all events, whether local or national, big or small. These events provide an excellent opportunity to expand your network, gain knowledge through trainings from experts and a source of motivation and inspiration that all add up to facilitate in maximizing duplication. Events also help in building your team dynamics and fostering a sense of unity and belongingness by bringing team members together.

Accelerate your business growth, don't miss the next event!

The FinFit Life **Model Business**

FinFit Life is the opportunity of a lifetime. It is the best part time income opportunity and can become one of the most profitable and scalable businesses in the marketplace today. What is a model business? It is a business that is efficient and effective continually produces prospects, teammates, business leaders, clients, and profit consistently. There are 3 parts to a model business:

- Meeting system
- Training System
- Financial Business operations system

Meeting System:

Having a system to follow is one of the most important things to have if you want to have predictable, efficient, and prosperous results. We all operate in this philosophy. All you must do is review your morning routine. All highly successful people wake up at the same time daily and have a routine. That routine is something like brushing their teeth, something fitness related, having coffee and breakfast, doing something in personal development and then launching their day. If you go into an office for work you probably drive to work the same way at the same time in a very efficient way, so much that I bet you don't even think about it to the point you may say you don't even remember driving to work. Our system has the same routine. It's our seven steps:

1.   Preparation

2.   Identify your target market

3.   Contact that market

4.   Share the company story

5.   Follow up answering questions and building relationships

6.   The Fast Start

7.   Repeat the process.

The leader leads and follows the meeting system that is throughout our system. The meeting system focuses on the following areas:

- Having a corporate overview meeting (Step 4) usually done twice a week on a Tuesday or Wednesday and a Thursday or Saturday in a webinar format – this is focused on telling the company story, the opportunity to build an income and/or how to become financially fit using our products and services how to become.

- Having a follow up meeting done 1 on 1 within 48 hours of the corporate overview. This is focused on answering questions, seeing if the candidate is a good fit for your business and getting a commitment to follow the process of our system.

- Fast Start Meeting that is focused on building a relationship, showing the associate how our products produce financial fitness for them and after getting them plugged into our training system (see the next section)

- Business grand opening meeting focusing on the newly licensed associate's grand opening of their business to all their family, friends, and business associates. It is designed to notify all that they are in business and what their business does so they can get referrals and potentially clients and new teammates.

- Big event meetings to share best practices from other leaders around the country.
    - National Conferences held 2 times a year focused on showing the size and strength of the FinFit Life opportunity and recognize those with high performance.
    - Regionally and locally called super Saturdays that does the same as the national meetings but with all local leaders.

Training System

- Set up team/baseshop training meetings weekly for everyone and for those that are more serious and licensed a Saturday meeting focused on leadership development, client presentations, and the FinFit Life product offering.
- Field training which is one on one with a new associate working with their referrals and potential clients. The focus is to show the associate how we teach financial fitness and implement the FinFit Life financial products that help families become financially fit.
- Big event training designed to develop leadership, system disciplines and business acumen.

Business Operations System

- Establishing a structured business schedule to have a prosperous life and business.
  - Business time (calls, meetings, training, appointments, etc.)
  - Family time
  - Personal development time
  - Faith
- Business operations for finances
  - 3 months of personal and business expenses
  - Open a credit card only for business expenses.
  - Potentially hire a bookkeeper for taxes

Main focuses are getting into the right market, building relationship, and gaining commitment with teammates.

7-point prospects

- 25 years old+
- Married
- Children
- Homeowner
- 50K+ income
- Entrepreneurial Minded
- Dissatisfied with current situation.

Signs you are running a model business.

1.   Attracting 10+ new teammates a month

2.   Helping 10+ families a month

3.   Having 10+ teammates at your weekly training

4.   Earning 10K or more per month of revenue

Master Constant Personal Communication

You must master the art of Constant Personal Communication to maximize your chances for success.

There are three types of communication you need to have with your leaders:

Constant Personal Motivation

Give praise when someone does well and encourage them when they are down.

You should communicate almost daily with your key leaders during their first two years--whether they are a thousand miles away or in the same city. This type of communication can mean everything to your team's success. Your role is to be a vision stretcher, not a problem-solver.

Constant Personal Information

Everyone loves good news - share it. With technology and the Internet, sharing current news and information to large masses of people has never been easier. However, it still takes a leader to make sure his/her team is receiving and processing this information on a timely basis. Make sure your leaders are constantly receiving information through every possible method:
- The FinFit Life website and social media
- Conference calls
- Webinars
- Events and meetings
- Personal correspondence –emails, phone calls, and team newsletters

Constant Personal Education

Leaders must make sure that their team members have the confidence and skills to take their game to the next level. You must run a system that is focused on regularly teaching the skills and abilities required to build your team members' FinFit Life business and client base.

Make sure your leaders are taking advantage of every educational opportunity possible:

- Sharing techniques through personal phone calls
- Field training
- Webinars
- Team training
- Local meetings and events
- Company events

Communication is the key to building a giant FinFit Life team. You must give your leaders the high-energy motivation and constant communication they need to build their business.

Become a "Director of Motivation"

Motivating your leaders does not mean you have to be the team's sole source of motivation.

All you have to do is become a "Director of Motivation" – someone who directs his people to the places, people, and events that will stretch their vision to see the endless possibilities.

There are two things you must remember:

1. People will rise no higher than their level of vision.
2. People will only change after having a significant emotional experience.

Every meeting and event at FinFit Life should focus on creating the perfect environment for vision-stretching and creating significant emotional experiences. History has proven that many of the legends in our business heard or felt something at a big event that caused them to believe they could become a huge success.

What if you or one of your leaders missed just one meeting, but it was the one that could have made the difference in making or breaking your career?

- You must commit to doing whatever it takes to attend every meeting and make sure that every member of your team does the same.
- Your business is built from great event to great event.
- You can always measure the success of a leader by who and how many follow him/her to great events. As soon as an event is announced, you must immediately begin promoting it to your entire team in all of your communications.

Meeting Cycle:

1. Corporate Overviews lead to local Training Events
2. Local Training Events lead to Big Company Events
3. Big Company Events lead to Massive Success!

Key Points to Teach Your Team How to Maximize the Power of All Events

1. Arrive prepared – attitude and appearance mean everything.
2. Take notes – you must be a student of the business.
3. Arrive early, stay late. You and your team can show your commitment by arriving early and taking the front seats. It is a very different meeting when you are in the front, instead of sitting in the back.
4. Commit to being the most excited team at the event.
5. Do not leave the meeting or hang out in the hallways.
6. Make sure to have a team recap meeting within the first few days of returning from an event to share the good news with people who were unable to attend.

History has shown that the leader who has the most people at most events will make the most money. Make sure you and your leaders become an effective and focused "Director of Motivation."

The Power of Local Training Events

Some of the most exciting meetings are local Training Events, offered at various times throughout the year. Training Events offer a dynamic format for information, education, inspiration, and recognition.

Key Points about Local Training Events

1. The main purpose of local Training Events is to share the vision of FinFit Life.
2. You should have the most enthusiastic and Do-It-First Leaders in the program.
3. Make sure you have a first-class location with an exciting and professional atmosphere.

Running a Local Training Event

One of the main responsibilities of a FinFit Life leader is coordinating and running high-powered local Training Events. Here are the keys to running a successful event:

1. Schedule the meeting two to four times a year.

2. Use only approved handouts and training materials.

3. Provide name badges for the event with the first names in large letters so speakers can see them easily.

4. Use motivational music for the walk-in and for breaks.

5. Use FinFit Life banners and multimedia to create the right atmosphere

6. Use the latest company videos and/or CORPORATE OVERVIEW to add even more excitement to the event.

7. Make sure your speakers are always enthusiastic, well prepared and focused.

8. Use your best local leaders to speak at your event, and bring in guest speakers when possible. There have always been two speaker rules in this industry that hold true:

    a. A prophet has no honor in his own land.

    b. The expert is someone who lives more than 150 miles away.

    This means that no matter how good a leader you are, it is always important to invite leaders from other areas who are aligned with the system to come in as guest speakers and teach your people.

9. The emcee should be dynamic, knowledgeable, and entertaining, with an ability to build on what the speakers say, as well as, add their own guidance.

10. Prepare a strong agenda and use it to stay on time when you hold the event.

FinFit Life **Technology**

Technology is constantly changing the world in which we live in. It changes our habits and the way we communicate with one another. With that in mind, FinFit Life is committed to maximizing your chances for success by integrating the latest technology to take us where things are heading, not where they are now or have been.

FinFit Life provides its associates with cutting-edge tools and training to help harness the power of the latest technologies in building your business. You can use these tools to enhance all or just certain parts of your business. You could even build a FinFit Life business from home as you master the tools and training provided.

Tools include:

- Robust, Mobile-Enabled Corporate Public Site
- Dynamic Corporate Social Media Pages- Facebook, Instagram, LinkedIn and TikTok
- FinFit Life Back-Office Support
- State-of-the-art online training platform at learn.finfitlife.com
- Corporate Text and Email Alerts
- FinFit Life Email Accounts to Licensed Associates
- Downloadable brochures and presentations that are email and text friendly
- E-Sign-up procedures for signing up Associates with FinFit Life
- E-Applications for writing business.
- Up-to-date business production reports and scoreboards
- Webinars for online Corporate Overviews, Fast Start Interviews, and Video links for recruiting and sales.

You will see these tools woven throughout this manual and in all the training that we do. Even though all the functions of the FinFit Life Business System can be done in a virtual environment, you should remember that FinFit Life uses a warm market system and does not believe in the spamming of mobile numbers or email addresses where there is no existing relationship.

We challenge you to not let technology scare you. Embrace it. We are here to help!

World-Class **Support**

FinFit Life provides world-class support to help its Associates succeed and build the business of their dreams. Just a few of the many support systems in place include:

The FinFit Life Headquarters

Based in Tampa Bay, Florida, the FinFit Life Headquarters has an executive and administrative team that is second to none. They are there to support you in all your marketing and building efforts.

Key email addresses to use include:

- General Questions? **info@FinFitLife .com**
- Agent Onboarding & Training Questions? **Onboarding@FinFitLife .com**
- Licensing and Carrier Appointment Question? **Licensing@FinFitLife .com**
- Commission Questions? **Commissions@finfitlife.com**
- Promotion Requests? **Promotions@finfitlife.com**

The headquarters team promptly returns all email inquiries within two business days.

World-Class **Events**

FinFit Life believes that you build a team and a company from big event to big event. The company hosts two major events each year to help you build your business

FinFit Life Launch Meeting - Kickstart your year on the right note with the FinFit Life Launch Meeting! Held at the onset of each year, this pivotal gathering is more than just a meeting—it's an energizing launchpad for all your ambitions and aspirations. Whether you're a seasoned member or a newcomer, the FinFit Life Launch Meeting is your best opportunity to align, inspire, and propel yourself to a year of unparalleled success.

FinFit Life Inspire Convention - Held each summer, the FinFit Life Inspire Convention is the premier event of the year! With the latest in training, motivation, recognition and inspiration, this event will fast-forward a person's career by 6-12 months.

The event is supercharged with special guest speakers, bombshell announcements, recognition of our semiannual leaders in recruiting, production, and leadership, and much more.

FinFit Life 5k Events – Whether you like to run, walk, or crawl this fun event is for you! Twice a year we hold a 5K event, typically in April and October, to bring awareness to our customers and associates of the importance of keeping a healthy and active lifestyle. Any money raised during the event is donated to a chosen charity and we love the opportunity of doing something together for a cause. We have locations setup from Hawaii to Florida to help grow the FinFit Life movement.

FinFit Life Weekly Live Trainings – Don't miss out on our weekly live trainings over Zoom. Links available in the Agent Portal and on the Training portal at learn.finfitlife.com.

Other Company Events (Live and Online) & Tours - These events are full of training, motivation, recognition, and inspiration. They are amazing events to use to recommit and prepare yourself and your team to succeed.

In Closing: **This is Our Promise to You**

FinFit Life will always:

- Be a professional company you can be proud of
- Be there to help you succeed
- Treat you with respect and integrity
- Give you the opportunity to help others improve their health, while saving and making more money
- Provide you the chance to build a great quality of life
- Give you the chance to become financially independent
- Finally, give you the chance to take charge of your life once and for all!

Nevertheless, we cannot do it for you. You provide the dreams and the work, and we provide the opportunity and the examples of success. The rest is up to you.

FinFit Life Business Building Blueprint
Index of Forms

The FinFit Life F-5 Worksheet

FAMILY	By When	FINANCES	By When	FRIENDS	By When	FITNESS	By When	FUN	By When

PERSONAL INTRINSIC PHILOSOPHY That which makes YOU --> YOU

My Purpose What do I want to do with my time on this planet	My Stand How do I validate my purpose (the way I do thing)	My Strengths Skill sets I possess that will enable me to fulfill my purposes and F-5 goals	Spoken Epitaph What I want people to say about me at my funeral
If you had the power to erase a regret in your life, what would you erase? Why?	Who is the person (living or not) whom you hold with the greatest respect? Why?	If you won the lottery tomorrow, what would you do with the money? Why?	If you were diagnosed with a terminal illness, what would you do with your final year?

Your F-5 Core Mission Statement is your WHY. Identifying & combining your F-5 Core Values & Personal Philosophy Into a single statement of action, which unifies your life mission fueling the confidence, resolve & fortitude to overcome adversity in the creation of a Bullet Proof Business Plan.

_____

_____

_____

_____

_____

_____

AN EXAMPLE OF AN AGENT'S F-5 TO HELP YOU GET STARTED

FAMILY	By When	FINANCES	By When	FRIENDS	By When	FITNESS	By When	FUN	By When
Devote more time to my daughter	Now	Pay off credit cards	1 yr	Pay total cost of my 25 year class reunion	4 yrs	Drop 5% body fat	1 yr	See my birthplace	5 yrs
Begin her retirement account	Now	Pay off cars	3 yrs	Golf trip to Scotland	4 yrs	Read more monthly	Now	Fit Camp	1 yr
		Pay off house	5 yrs					Dream Boat	5 yrs

PERSONAL INTRINSIC PHILOSOPHY That which makes YOU --> YOU

My Purpose	My Stand	My Strengths	Spoken Epitaph
What do I want to do with my time on this planet	How do I validate my purpose (the way I do thing)	Skill sets I possess that will enable me to fulfill my purposes and F-5 goals	What I want people to say about me at my funeral
Be the driving force for my family	Do it right the first time	Tenacity	He lead by example
Inspire others to improve	Authentic speak	Leadership	He lived a life that others dream of
Become a role model	Think BIG	Organization	He provided for his family
Show my daughter the way to success	Find a way to win	Enthusiasm	He was a true teammate
If you had the power to erase a regret in your life, what would you erase? Why?	Who is the person (living or not) whom you hold with the greatest respect? Why?	If you won the lottery tomorrow, what would you do with the money? Why?	If you were diagnosed with a terminal illness, what would you do with your final year?
My career choice	Abraham Lincoln	Pay off all my debt	Seek to repair relationships
Apologize to my first wife	He was relentless is his pursuit of his dreams of success even though he failed many times over many different ventures. He took a stand against tyranny and the exploits of the status quo to do the right thing for people other than himself at the greatest cost.	Pay off my parents debt	Spend more time with family
Not serving my country		Begin an IRA for my children	Finally sky dive
Took my family for granted		Take a year off to sail around the world	Find my father
Picking on someone in school		Start a scholarship for veterans	

Your F-5 Core Mission Statement is your WHY. Identifying & combining your F-5 Core Values & Personal Philosophy Into a single statement of action, which unifies your life mission fueling the confidence, resolve & fortitude to overcome adversity in the creation of a Bullet Proof Business Plan.

My mission is to lead from the front of the line. To utilize my gifts of teaching and leadership to create opportunities and advantages for those that are close to me as well as some that have never heard of me. With my skill set and opportunity laid before me, I am in a unique position to push my physical and mental limitation to greater level of awareness and lift those up around me who I wish to help and who are in need_ I would like to stop paying interest to the bank and create investments which they pay interest to me. I have a burning desire to help some of my close friends with services that are important to them that will altruistically benefit others. To create residual income streams that will benefit my legacy.

BUSINESS BLUEPRINT QUANTIFYING TOOL
Establish what you want, for whom you want it, & what it is going to take to achieve it. **THINK BIG** *you will be surprised how achievable your dreams may be.*

Family
Buy new house, car, boat, clothes, College Funding, Vacation, and More Free Time

What are some items/activates you want for your family?			
Items/Action	Time	Investment	Money

Finances
Spouse can quit job, supplement retirement strategy, pay off credit card debt, and consolidate student loans

What are some things you want accomplish to improve your financial position?			
Items/Action	Time	Investment	Money

Friends
Wives Trip to Caribbean, Husbands Scotland golf trip, National Championship trip, and Concerts

What are some things you want to do socially with friends?			
Items/Action	Time	Investment	Money

Fitness
Athletic Competition, College, Write a Book, reduce BMI and Train for a marathon

What activities/items do you need to do to be able to increase your fitness?			
Items/Action	Time	Investment	Money

FUN
Become a Big Brother/Sister, Sky Diving, Quit Smoking, Lose Weight, Volunteer, or Travel

List activities you want to accomplish for yourself that will be fun before you die.			
Items/Action	Time	Investment	Money

What needs to happen to reach your goals:

_____

_____

_____

Memory Jogger

Use the FinFit Memory Jogger to help come up with potential prospects in your network!

WHO DO YOU KNOW THAT:

Wants to save money	Wants to make extra money	Is Entrepreneurial
Quit their job	Wants a healthier lifestyle	Is a Fitness Advocate
Works in healthcare	Is tech Savvy	

WHO ARE YOUR FAMILY AND FRIENDS:

Parents	In-Laws	Sisters & Brothers	Sister & Brother-In-Laws	Accountant
Aunts & Uncles	Cousins	Grandparents	Best Man at wedding	IT Service Person
Bridesmaids	Neighbors	College Friends	Nanny	Nieces & Nephews
Gym Friends	Boss/Partner	Work Associates	Manager/Supervisor	Maid of Honor
Co-Worker	Receptionist	Landlord	Personal Manager	Church Friends

WHO HAS A SPECIAL JOB OR INTEREST:

Accountant	Burials	Glass	Mortgage	Relocation
Advertising	Cabinets	Golf	Motel	Rental
Airline Employee	Carpet	Grocers	Motorcycles	Restaurant
Apartment	Caterers	Hair	Motor Homes	Retirement
Manager	Childcare	Health	Movers	Satellite
Appliances	Church	Heating & Air	Movies	School
Appraisers	Computers	Hobby	Music	Security
Architects	Consultant	Hospital	Newspapers	Signs
Artist	Contractor	Hotel	Nursery	Ski
Attorney	Crafts	Insurance	Nursing	Soccer
Auditor	Dance	Internet	Optical	Spas
Auto Detailing	Delivery	Landscape	Party Planner	Storage
Auto Parts	Electric	Laundry	Payroll	Plays sports
Auto Repairing	Engineer	Lawn	Pet Business	Taxes
Auto Sales	Executive	Lighting	Photographers	Telecommunications
Baker	Exercise	Limousine	Piano	Telephone
Beauty	Financing	Loans	Pizza	Television
Consultant	Fire	Locks	Plumbing	Theatre
Bicycles	Florists	Mail	Police	Towing
Boats	Funeral	Martial Arts	Printers	Travel
Books	Furniture	Management	Radio	Truck
Bridal	Gifts	Massage	Real Estate	University

FINFIT LIFE

TOP 25 List

My Name: _____
Date Completed: _____

My Director: _____
Sent to Director: _____

	First Name	Last Name	R/F/A*	Phone Number	Profile**	FITNESS***	Characteristics	Hot Button	Contact Date	VIP Attendance	Results	Comments
1					□1 □2 □3 □4 □5 □6 □7 □8							
2					□1 □2 □3 □4 □5 □6 □7 □8							
3					□1 □2 □3 □4 □5 □6 □7 □8							
4					□1 □2 □3 □4 □5 □6 □7 □8							
5					□1 □2 □3 □4 □5 □6 □7 □8							
6					□1 □2 □3 □4 □5 □6 □7 □8							
7					□1 □2 □3 □4 □5 □6 □7 □8							
8					□1 □2 □3 □4 □5 □6 □7 □8							
9					□1 □2 □3 □4 □5 □6 □7 □8							
10					□1 □2 □3 □4 □5 □6 □7 □8							
11					□1 □2 □3 □4 □5 □6 □7 □8							
12					□1 □2 □3 □4 □5 □6 □7 □8							
13					□1 □2 □3 □4 □5 □6 □7 □8							
14					□1 □2 □3 □4 □5 □6 □7 □8							
15					□1 □2 □3 □4 □5 □6 □7 □8							
16					□1 □2 □3 □4 □5 □6 □7 □8							
17					□1 □2 □3 □4 □5 □6 □7 □8							
18					□1 □2 □3 □4 □5 □6 □7 □8							
19					□1 □2 □3 □4 □5 □6 □7 □8							
20					□1 □2 □3 □4 □5 □6 □7 □8							
21					□1 □2 □3 □4 □5 □6 □7 □8							
22					□1 □2 □3 □4 □5 □6 □7 □8							
23					□1 □2 □3 □4 □5 □6 □7 □8							
24					□1 □2 □3 □4 □5 □6 □7 □8							
25					□1 □2 □3 □4 □5 □6 □7 □8							

* R/F/A -- (R) relative   (F) friend   (A) acquaintance

** Profile -- 1. Over 25+ Years   2. Married   3. Children   4. Homeowner   5. Good Job/profession   6. Income over 35k   7. Dissatisfied   8. Entrepreneurial

***FITNESS -- 1. Fitness minded   2. Insurance industry   3. Teacher/coach/trainer   4. Network marketing   5. Enthusiastic   6. Sales   7. Self Employed

Confirmation List

My Name:	My Director:
Date Completed:	Director Review:

	First Name	Last Name	Phone Number	Email	Associate	Invited By
1						
2						
3						
4						
5						
6						
7						
8						
9						
10						
11						
12						
13						
14						
15						

The FinFit Life Website

Promo Site

Agent Portal

Training Portal

Get Appointed

Business Builder Toolkit

Support

Follow Us on Social

Glossary of Terms

Advanced Commissions - commissions that are paid to an agent as a loan or advance prior to the client making the payments to cover that commission.

Agent - someone who has joined FinFit Life and is licensed to do business.

As-Earned Commission - commissions that are paid to an agent as the client actually makes the payments to cover that commission.

Associate - someone who has joined FinFit Life. Also called a Member or Representative.

Base shop – the main business unit of a base shop leader. Includes all the Associates directly under a base shop leader before a team member qualifies to be a base shop leader and branches off to become his or her own base shop.

Base Shop Leader – once an Associate reaches the highest personal production compensation level and has his or her direct team.

Chargeback - a reversal of a commission to an agent caused by either non-payment or cancelation of their product.

Compensation Plan - a system that compensates consultants for their efforts and must be based primarily on the sales of products by the consultant and his/her downline. The level of earnings is often based on an achieved title or rank and is usually a percentage commission of sales. There are various types of compensation plans so it is important to fully understand how one will be compensated before joining a company.

Direct marketing - a method used to distribute advertising and marketing materials such as catalogs, brochures or other items to consumers through mail, e-mail, telemarketing or other methods. Direct selling is NOT direct marketing.

Downline - refers to a group of people that consultants bring into a company to generate sales, their Associates and so on.

FFA - abbreviation for Financial Fitness Associate or adviser

FinFit Life – shorthand for FinFit Life

Generations - leaders in your downline that have obtained the same contract as you and run their own base shops.

Group Presentation - live presentation made in an office or hotel to a group

Hierarchy - refers to the team members on a specific team.

Independent contractors - Persons who perform work or services for an entity on a non-employee basis. Direct sellers are statutory non-employees, and are treated as self-employed for all Federal tax purposes, including income and employment taxes, if: 1) all substantial payments for their services as direct sellers are directly related to sales or other outputs, rather than to the number of hours worked; and 2) their services are performed under a written contract providing that they will not be treated as employees for Federal tax purposes. FinFit Life field representatives are independent contractors.

Manufacturer/Product Provider - companies that provide and service products that are sold by marketing organizations like FinFit Life.

Member - someone who has joined FinFit Life. Also called an Associate or Representative.

Needs Analysis - a tool used to identify the financial needs of a potential client

One-on-One Presentation - live presentation made in a home, office, or restaurant to one person or, preferably, to a couple.

Online Presentation - live or recorded presentation conducted online

Override - the revenue that is earned from a production done by one of your team members

Products - Goods and services provided by product providers or manufacturers to marketing organizations like FinFit Life to be sold to the public. The products FinFit Life markets are financial in nature and include insurance, annuities and other financial products.

Relationship Marketing - Marketing that takes place in the warm markets of people where there is already an existing relationship whether it be friends, relatives, neighbors, co-workers, and other past and current business contacts.

Representative - someone who has joined and contracted with FinFit Life.

Single level compensation plan - structure in which a representative is compensated based solely on his or her individual product sales.

Sponsor - Someone who signs up a direct member. Also called a direct upline.

Target Premium - the commissionable portion of a Life insurance sale

Upline- refers to a consultant's sponsor, along with his/her sponsor, etc.

Made in the USA
Columbia, SC
14 November 2024

46526005R00073